THE LARGER EVILS

THE LARGER EVILS

NINETEEN EIGHTY-FOUR

●

THE TRUTH
BEHIND THE SATIRE

W.J. West

CANONGATE PRESS

First published in Great Britain in 1992 by
Canongate Press plc
14 Frederick Street
Edinburgh

British Library Cataloguing-in-Publication Data
A catalogue record for this book is available on request
from the British Library.

ISBN 0 86241 382 6

Typeset by Hewer Text Composition Services, Edinburgh
Printed and bound in Great Britain by Butler and Tanner Ltd, Frome

Acknowledgments

The extensive Orwell archive at University College London is an essential starting point for anyone seriously interested in George Orwell's work, and I am grateful for the assistance and help provided over several years by the archivist Gill Furlong and the staff. Perhaps the strongest holdings of Orwell material outside the Orwell archive itself are to be found at the BBC's Written Archive Centre at Caversham, Reading, along with some material by Orwell's first wife Eileen, and many other figures in Orwell's life. I am grateful to the staff there for their unfailing help and assistance. The other main source for material used here is the Public Record Offices at Kew, and at Chancery Lane, both invaluable. I should also like to thank the staff at the India Office Library, the libraries at the Devon and Exeter Institution, at College Green Bristol and Leicester Square Westminster, and the booksellers, particularly those supplying out-of-print books not readily to be found in the large national collections.

Of those who were close to Orwell on Jura I would particularly like to thank Bill Dunn who farmed with him there and Henry Dakin who took the oars when Orwell's boat was caught in the Corryvrekin whirlpool and who now has the Blair family bible with its family tree, and the portrait of Lady Mary Blair reproduced here. On Jura itself I would like to thank the Fletchers of Ardlussa who have preserved Barnhill where *Nineteen Eighty-Four* was written almost exactly as it was, and who kindly allowed me to use the library at Ardlussa.

Amongst many friends of Orwell I would like to thank particularly Tosco Fyvel, Douglas Cleverdon and Laurence Brander, all of whom have now, sadly, passed away, and John Atkins, Desmond Hawkins, Mulk Raj Anand, Mrs Celia Goodman, Lettice Cooper and also Leonard Miall and the late Mrs I. D. Benzie-Morley. Of those who have written about Orwell, not already mentioned, I am grateful for the comments and assistance given by Professor Peter Davison and for his edition of the extant manuscript of *Nineteen Eighty-Four* and, until the Davison edition of Orwell's works appears, have been very glad of the four volume *Collected Essays, Journalism and Letters* edited by Ian Angus. Similarly those who write about Orwell today will find themselves referring continually to the first biography of Orwell by Bernard Crick, as I have done with gratitude. There have been many others who have offered advice and assistance, particularly after the appearance of the BBC Orwell scripts in 1984. I am grateful for their help and the help of those already mentioned whilst making it plain that the opinions expressed in this book and the conclusions are my responsibility alone.

Finally I would like to thank my editor at Canongate, Lorraine McCann, for her helpful suggestions and my publisher, Stephanie Wolfe Murray, whose never failing enthusiasm has carried the book along from the first.

Contents

To the Islanders of Jura

It was not desirable that the proles should have strong political feelings. All that was required of them was a primitive patriotism which could be appealed to whenever it was necessary to make them accept longer working hours or shorter rations. And even when they became discontented, as they sometimes did, their discontent led nowhere, because being without general ideas, they could only focus it on petty specific grievances. The larger evils invariably escaped their notice.

from *Nineteen Eighty-Four*

Preface

The discovery of new work by a foremost author is always exciting; when it leads to the discovery of yet further material on a scale which overthrows accepted wisdom on one of the masterworks of an era then the excitement is lifted to a new plane. A biographer rarely has such an opportunity and it has only happened here through the discovery at the BBC, in 1984 itself, of a large cache of Orwell texts, letters and memoranda. This material was published shortly afterwards but a wealth of related material from the same archive was only hinted at. More importantly the BBC material as a whole provided the key which enabled other archives to be unlocked which complemented Orwell's own writings. It filled out the picture with new material that concerned the world in which he lived and which created *Nineteen Eighty-Four*.

The work of discovery in the archives, mostly dealing with censorship and secret domestic politics in Britain, took some years. It in turn led to literary sources and to people who had known Orwell or been involved in the world *Nineteen Eighty-Four* satirised. Finally, a wider picture began to emerge of what Orwell's masterwork had been about. The published biographies were completely ignorant of the greater part of this new material so it was obviously essential to write an account of it that would establish a new biographical framework for the all-important later years of Orwell's life when he wrote *Nineteen Eighty-Four* and *Animal Farm*.

A biographer looking at Orwell's work today is faced

with many questions that are still unanswered, despite the appearance of the authorised and many unofficial biographies. The average readers want one thing above all others: they want to know all there is to know about *Nineteen Eighty-Four*. How did Orwell come to write one of the most important books of the twentieth century? Why did the book have the success it did, which came as a surprise to Orwell himself who thought it might sell 10,000 copies rather than the millions which finally spilled from the presses? Sadly these questions have never been focused on. There has been a tendency to treat all Orwell's works equally, even books which he thought of as pot-boilers and which he asked should not be reprinted. This may seem the logical approach to literary critics trying to cast Orwell in the mould of a nineteenth-century classic author who just happened to have his two last books catch the public imagination. The ordinary reader who knows Orwell from *Nineteen Eighty-Four* would disagree with this approach. He would think surely there *must* be something special about such a book. And he would be right.

What is revealed now are the true origins of Orwell's great work. They include the first account of the role Orwell's wife Eileen played in the development of the book—it has long been known that she was involved in the planning and writing of *Animal Farm* but her connection with *Nineteen Eighty-Four* has not been suspected. She worked in a highly secret world in wartime London which gave her access to knowledge which complemented Orwell's gained through his work at the BBC. The book then looks at the world Orwell lived in, the arguments with friends and other authors that formed the intellectual under-pinning of his work; and most importantly the books he read. We know a lot about these, partly because of his reviews, but also through many of the books themselves which have survived in the Orwell archive. Yet it is this aspect of Orwell's intellectual life that has been most neglected by his biographers up until now. It takes considerable time to read through the works of such people as John Middleton

Murry, now a forgotten figure to the general reading public, but Orwell read his many books and reacted to them strongly. No biography which does not follow the same path can begin to approach its subject with any conviction.

Another literary factor almost entirely neglected by earlier commentators is the importance of American influence on Orwell, both through the reading of such works as Jack London's *The Iron Heel* and his connection with American letters in magazines such as *Partisan Review*. These influences were heightened by facts about Orwell's family background revealed for the first time here which made him seem to some more a New Englander than an Englishman, certainly someone with an American's view of freedom.

With so much known about Orwell, an author who has been in the public eye for so long, it perhaps needs explaining how the roots of *Nineteen Eighty-Four* have remained largely undetected for so long, and why the various biographers who have written about Orwell have failed to uncover them, despite the most recent having been written after the discovery of the first Orwell BBC material.

The reasons are two-fold and of interest to modern historians as well as those with a simple biographical interest in Orwell. First, Orwell's early death at the age of forty-six, in the year after the publication of *Nineteen Eighty-Four*, created a very unusual situation. We have been deprived of other works which would have given us the full flowering of his art, and we have also been deprived of his comments on *Nineteen Eighty-Four* over the years and his views on what the world was making of it. Had he lived only a few more years we would have had his comments on the defection of Guy Burgess to Russia. Burgess had been a close working colleague of Orwell's, as we shall see, and represented a great deal in the British political and arts establishment that Orwell was fighting against although he had no way of knowing this at the time. The enemy had been far closer than he knew. By the time 1984 arrived Orwell would have been eighty-one. He cannot have expected to live that long but he might have hoped that others near him would have been able to explain his book, and the world it was satirising, as time passed and the inevitable distortions crept in.

This did not happen. In the end it was almost as if the book had been written many years before and was already a classic ready-made when it appeared. Classed from the first alongside Huxley's *Brave New World* and the earlier classics of H. G. Wells, the massive success of the book which carried on through to 1984 and beyond seemed to have lifted it out of the normal historical processes and placed it at one bound alongside works such as Swift's *Gulliver's Travels*. And this raises the second reason for biographers failing to come to grips with the book: the role of many of those who knew Orwell and even lived on to see the climactic year of 1984. Why had they not been able to make any significant comment on the roots of Orwell's masterwork?

It is difficult now to recapture the spirit of political controversy that surrounded Orwell's book in the post-war years. On the left in Britain *Nineteen Eighty-Four* was widely condemned, even as it was selling in its hundreds of thousands. It was said to be a cold war text, one of the most violently partisan in battles which determined the shape of post-war Britain and the failure, as many of them saw it, of a true far-left regime to be established in Britain. It was in those years that many of the stories about Orwell began and the established view of him amongst the literary establishment in Britain, but not in America, was laid down. Stories were told to prove a point; anecdotes about him focused on incidents which gave a misleading impression and the idea was created that, in literary terms, he was not really very important and his book would soon fade. Those telling the stories who professed to be close friends of Orwell's were at best colleagues or lunchtime drinking companions, the very people that Orwell had to go to Jura to avoid so that he could write his book in peace. To be sure it was only the actual communists and fellow-travellers that launched full-blown attacks on Orwell and *Nineteen Eighty-Four*, and these continued right up to 1984 itself, only faltering with the fall of the regimes in the East. But people who loudly proclaimed their closeness to him more often than not damned his work with faint praise. Orwell's very success made him suspect and it was the fashion to decry his fiction, the only reason for his fame, and to divert attention to his journalism for papers such as *Tribune* as being the 'real' Orwell.

It was not until the sixties that the weight of this hostility amongst some of the influential intellectuals began to lift; by then the traumas of the defection of Burgess and the Philby scandal and other problems much closer to home—the role of people such as Claud Cockburn, Maurice Webb, Tom Driberg, Francis Williams and Kingsley Martin and his circle—had passed. But questions which should have been asked were forgotten; the legend had already begun to take hold. The development of Orwell's reputation followed the same paths any historian or biographer would recognise. Perceptions changed, memories faded, half-truth became truth and fiction was often accepted as fact. Examples will be found throughout this book and it is a measure of the extent of them that the BBC material should have remained unknown and even unsuspected for so long when many of those who took part in Orwell's programmes were still alive. When the scripts and talks were discovered, and those who had taken part interviewed, they seemed almost to be learning for the first time of events they had completely forgotten. Despite their often great interest in Orwell it had never occurred to them that the archives still kept their original material—or that it should not have been known that they had. In nearly every case they had watched Orwell's reputation grow with the decades and had to come to terms with this and their own memories of the man. Despite their often close knowledge the memories proved fragile in the face of the legend, and after all they had only seen part of his life. Their reaction to the original material from forty and fifty years before was to plunge them back into their own lives and in some cases to hope that some fresh work might be written to establish the new perspective, another reason for writing the present book. It is a rare person indeed who can retain their vision clear across half a century.

Less understandable than the failings of human memory are such facts as the connection between Orwell and Guy Burgess. How *could* a direct connection between two such prominent figures in modern British life have remained unknown for so long? The answer, developed here, points to the struggle Orwell had to go through during his lifetime and also to the real problems contemporary historians are going to have in writing a proper account of post-war British political and literary history, despite what seems to be universal record keeping and a plethora of source material.

A central figure in the shaping of the Orwell legend was undoubtedly Orwell's second wife Sonia. She lived until 1980 and was the driving force behind the setting up of the Orwell archive and also the co-editor of the four volumes of collected essays and letters which were intended to stand in place of a biography. She stuck as long as possible to Orwell's injunction in his will that no biography be written. However, her position was essentially a tragic one. She had married Orwell on his death bed, quite literally, in circumstances which many have found difficult to understand. It was well known at the time, though forgotten now, that people in the last stages of tuberculosis frequently formed very strong emotional attachments, indeed those visiting patients were warned against the danger of taking such relationships at their face value. There is no evidence that Orwell knew Sonia in the wartime years as anything other than a secretary at the magazine *Horizon* run by his friend Cyril Connolly. He was attracted to her but when he asked her to come to Jura for a visit she declined to do so. She appeared again only in the last days.

Whatever the connection between them that led to the marriage, it was only after Orwell's death that she became involved with him to such an extent that she used the name Sonia Orwell—even Orwell had never changed his family name from Blair and tended to use Blair exclusively in his private life towards the end, and on Jura. She did not herself look after Orwell's son, as he might well have thought she would, but she did jealously guard his literary identity. In doing so she inevitably drew attention away from the far more important figure of Eileen, Orwell's first wife. It is not the least part of this book's aim to correct that imbalance. If Orwell's death at forty-six was a tragedy then Eileen's was ever more of one, for she did not even reach forty. She was indeed a heroic figure; had she survived, much of what is described in this book would surely have been known already. Her eclipse in the public's mind by Orwell's widow is understandable but it has played no small part in the mystery which has arisen over Orwell and the roots of his most famous book.

Orwell did of course have other friends who were not part of the far-left literary establishment in post-war Britain. However they, like him, were on the defensive and tended to be 'real people' who lived largely private lives. One wartime friend, who never talked to any biographer, told the author that he had thought of setting up an 'Orwell Protection Society' but ironically it was the establishment in Britain who took this line, protesting that Orwell's body had been hijacked for political purposes by American critics and their sympathisers in Britain. Many of those who have taken this line will be shocked to discover here that they have been defending people who actually banned *Animal Farm* and other works of Orwell's at the time and would have been very happy if *Nineteen Eighty-Four* had never been published. But such home truths are always hard to face.

There was a group, described later in detail, around John Middleton Murry, who no doubt knew what Orwell was attacking very well but did not defend him because they thought he had betrayed them—they were people who shared Orwell's earlier pacifism but did not reject it as he did when war came. One such couple was Reg Reynolds and his wife Ethel Mannin. After the war Reynolds edited a two-volume collection of British political pamphlets with Orwell. Orwell had known him as the man who had approached the British government in India on Gandhi's behalf before the war and they shared many friends, yet Reynolds is not mentioned in any of the biographies of Orwell. During the war Orwell was often seen with Ethel Mannin—who seems also to have been a friend of Eileen's—but nothing further has been discovered about their relationship or the intellectual relationship between Orwell and Reynolds which must have been of some substance. Perhaps Orwell's betrayal, as they saw it, of their pacifist ideals kept them from speaking as his reputation and its distortions grew. Orwell edited other texts with Tosco Fyvel during the war, and, as we shall describe, wrote a book jointly with Inez Holden, who is a very plausible model of Julia in *Nineteen Eighty-Four*, and with both he had strong connections. They both spoke up for him.

Modern historians reading the account of Orwell's world here will be struck by the way Orwell's satire has provided a genuine understanding of the kind of realities which are most difficult to uncover. The facts about radio propaganda and censorship have been dealt with in America by Lawrence C. Soley's *Radio Warfare: OSS and CIA Subversive Propaganda* (1989) and I have dealt with similar material in *Truth Betrayed: Radio and Politics Between the Wars* (1987). However the overview of the subject here, and its importance for Orwell's quasi-totalitarian world in *Nineteen Eighty-Four*, is entirely new. There was nothing in American experience quite so Orwellian as the Anti-Lie Bureau at the Ministry of Information. Had Orwell lived in America he would not perhaps have needed to write the warning he did; historians can be grateful that his struggles produced valid insights, written at the time, which are of direct help to us now.

CHAPTER ONE

Introduction

The revelations following the collapse of the communist regimes in Eastern Europe in the 1990s confirmed what had been obvious to intelligent critics of those regimes for many years. Life in the 'iron curtain' countries had been harsh, except for a few privileged party members; there had been massive security supervision of everyone both inside and outside the system; and finally the entire system had been based on fear rather than the creation of a state based on brotherly love and the brotherhood of man. George Orwell's *Nineteen Eighty-Four*, criticised for generations by communist intellectuals as being absurd and others as being an exaggerated fantasy by a terminally ill man, proved to be a precisely accurate account of a bureaucratic totalitarian state. And Orwell had specifically said that his book was a parody, a satire of something which *could* happen in Britain if people were not vigilant.

Satire only works well if the reader comes to see fully what is being satirised in the world about him. He may not at first see the grain of truth amongst the absurdidites but when he does it must strike hard. People in the East have seen the force of what Orwell was saying in *Nineteen Eighty-Four*. For them he has caught not just one grain of truth but many.

The problem some in the West have found with *Nineteen Eighty-Four* as a satire is that they cannot immediately see the grain of truth, and the convulsive laughter with which the great satires such as Swift's *Gulliver's Travels* are read is entirely absent. It would be a strange reader who could find something to laugh at in Orwell's masterpiece in any chapter, let alone on every page. The book resembles far more strongly a deliberate cold warning of the kind seen in Jack London's *The Iron Heel*, a book which did indeed provide Orwell with much of the original inspiration for *Nineteen Eighty-Four*.

An explanation of this paradox is attempted in this book. Orwell's warning will be shown to be based on a savage satire of a world which actually existed in Britain, but a secret world rather than a public one, a world, moreover, which many intellectuals in Britain did not find uncongenial. All the elements found in the hated Stasi regime in East Germany were to be found in this world in embryo, and there is still a totalitarian streak running through the inner bureaucracy in Britain today. Orwell's fears about the spread of totalitarianism were very much those of a man who believed in freedom and a kind of freedom which is found more often in America than it is in Britain. It was no accident that he was inspired by Jack London or that some of his best essays were written for the American magazine *Partisan Review* or, finally, that his book and its message were appreciated immediately there on a far greater scale than in Britain itself. Orwell wrote in his book *The Lion and the Unicorn*:

> The whole English-speaking world is haunted by the idea of human equality, and though it would simply be a lie to say that either we or the Americans have ever acted up to our professions, still, the *idea* is there, and it is capable of one day becoming a reality. From the English-speaking culture, if it does not perish, a society of free and equal human beings will ultimately arise.

It is clear from this that he thought of Britain and America as inextricably linked through their common culture. But his understanding of America and sympathy with what it stood for seen in those ultimate terms went beyond intellectual agreement. The Canadian writer Paul Potts wrote of Orwell:

2

He loved Nineteenth century America. Mark Twain could easily have been his favourite author. In many small things he was more like a New Englander then than an Englishman now . . . Orwell wasn't a creative writer of the first range. He did, however, write some very fine English prose, as good as Lincoln, Tom Paine and Jefferson.

Potts' comments are remarkably shrewd and make a point which few of Orwell's biographers, official or unofficial, have realised. In fact Orwell resembled a nineteenth-century New Englander because of his background which was rooted one century further back still, in the eighteenth century, when the Blairs first blazed a trail literally around the world. So important is this neglected dimension of Orwell's background that it is worth looking at it briefly, before going on to give some account of his own early life and the entirely new ground that will be covered in the rest of the book.

George Orwell was born Eric Arthur Blair in India where his father was an official in the Opium Department of the Indian Civil Service. The Blair family were known to have come from Scotland originally and then to have gone to Jamaica where their fortunes were made. The well-known photographs of Orwell taken in his flat in Islington show an eighteenth-century family portrait in the background. This portrait, which still survives, is of Lady Mary Blair, a daughter of the Earl of Westmorland, and ancestor of Orwell's. It has not been possible to trace the precise links between the different branches of the extensive Blair clan, however the last of the great land-owning Blairs, the Jamaica and India nabobs, was Lambert Blair who died in 1815. He had come home to England towards the end of his life, setting up home in Devon, near Exmouth, in a white house called Courtlands that he bought from one of the Baring brothers, founders of the famous banking house. When he died his will detailed his estates which included land in Jamaica but also in Surinam in the Dutch West Indies. The human face of the family is shown in his bequest to another Lambert Blair, described as a mulatto living in the West Indies. There is a record in Exeter of the baptism of a black woman from the West Indies living near Exmouth at this time; a servant of the Blairs', only her Christian names were given and it would seem likely that this was the mother of the mulatto Lambert Blair—the elder Lambert Blair of course had a wife in England who survived him. The bulk of his estate was left to Mark Blair, son of his brother John, who subsequently entered parliament and was one of the last spokesmen for the West Indian plantation owners. John Blair himself seems likely to be the same John Blair who appears in the East India Company records in 1790 as the first of the Blair family to work for them where he ran a pepper go-down (or factory) in Sarawak. Over a century later Orwell's father was one of many Blair descendants working in India. We see a family, rooted in the eighteenth century, who were classic nabobs, feeling far more at home in India or the West Indies or America than they would in Scotland or England, but nonetheless likely to come home at the end of their days.

On Orwell's mother's side there was the same pattern but with a base in Burma where the Limouzins, a French family, had had commercial interests going back well into the nineteenth century, if not before; a Limouzin burial place has been found in Burma dating from 1860. Ida Limouzin was born in England, her mother was English, but she was brought up in Moulmein in Burma where her father then ran a teak business. Orwell's grandmother Theresa Limouzin was still living in Moulmein when he went there as an officer in the Indian Imperial Police after leaving Eton in 1923.

Surviving members of Orwell's family have said to the author that they did not feel as if they *came from* anywhere and this was a common feeling in other families in the colonial world. The sense of freedom that this gave people often made the world of England seem more than a little parochial, the tone of life there completely lacking in any real sense of liberty. It was this feeling of freedom and independence that led, finally, to the Wars of Independence and the establishment of the United States. Such a world perspective, where a man might have property in Jamaica, and at the same time be at home in Surinam, with a brother in the India service, was reflected also in the literature of the time. Orwell was given a copy of *Gulliver's Travels* for his eighth birthday, he tells us in a later essay. When the book was published travels of this kind were not as fantastic as they seem to us now; they were the normal background to the lives of people such as the Blairs. Swift was writing a political satire: a John Blair might half seriously wonder if he could not guess where that island with its extraordinarily small people might be. And the book would have been a part of any well-read American's life just as it would of anyone in England. When Orwell left his school to go to Burma he was, in a sense, entering into his inheritance, but it was an inheritance that had become depleted and warped by the passage of time and he revolted against it. What he found, when he had pursued the tortuous path of revolt, was the same perspective as the American descendents of those eighteenth-century figures who, in their revolt, had perpetuated the original vision of the freedom found by his Blair forebears. Set against this were continental ideas which survived through to the twentieth century in their last developments and Orwell identified in a key quotation we shall see again—

The whole conception of the militarised continental state with its secret police, its censored literature and its conscript labour, is utterly different from that of the loose maritime democracy . . .

Ideas of this kind, this view of freedom, are profoundly different from those of Marxist or more conventional left-wing thinkers, and that they inspired Orwell accounted for a great deal of the differences between Orwell's thought and that of others on the left which had become widespread in Britain from the end of the nineteenth century onwards. They had not passed by even Eton where the problem of the rising proletariat was referred to as 'the Labour question'. In 1894 the left-wing thinker Geoffrey Drage lectured the school on 'Eton and the Labour Question'. And at this time the school set up a mission in the east end of London with the expressed aim of restoring the balance between the haves and the have nots. Eton boys were encouraged to spend some of their time helping with this mission work and Orwell may well have done so, although no records of the work were kept. When Orwell returned from Burma and began his descent into the world which Jack London described in *The People of the Abyss* he might have been doing more than following in London's footsteps as he later said he had done. He might himself once have been on the other side of the fence as an Eton schoolboy extending a charitable hand.

Many authors have puzzled over why Orwell should have chosen to write under a pseudonym rather than his own name. One story that sounds plausible had him disagreeing with his father over the book he was writing and choosing the name because they were walking near the river Orwell, and George was a very English name. This may have been true, it has the ring of truth about it, but it does not explain to a modern reader why there should be the need. The answer almost certainly goes back to Orwell's days at Eton. To have written *Down and Out in Paris and London* under his own name would have brought immediate disgrace to his family and perhaps even legal complications. That this fear was not an idle one can be seen from the reaction of Orwell's tutor at Eton, Andrew S. F. Gow, when he found out during the war who 'George Orwell' was. Writing in a circular newsletter to his old pupils from both Eton and Cambridge, where he subsequently went, he described some of his light reading matter:

I have also read *Down and Out* [sic] by G. Orwell (a pseudonym) not because washing up dishes in Parisian restaurants appeals to me much but because the author was my pupil, though not in this subject.

It appears that Gow came to regret this snide comment, for he visited Orwell on his death bed, but the reaction of someone who was close to Orwell, who had by this time made a considerable name for himself in serious journalism, shows just how impossible it would have been to use his own name.

After Orwell emerged from his days down and out and learnt to swim in the left-wing literary subculture of London life in the thirties he took what turned out to be a decisive step in his life, as it is in most people's, when he decided to get married. His wife was Eileen O'Shaughnessy, an Oxford graduate in English, although at first she studied theology, who came originally from Sunderland. Her effect on Orwell's work was profound and forms a major theme in this book; her experience of the totalitarian world of wartime London was as extensive as Orwell's whilst her influence on the actual style and structure of his last two works was also considerable.

Soon after they were married Eileen learnt that her life was going to be dominated by three things: Orwell's interest in politics, his work as a writer, and his health. His interest in politics became all consuming at the time of the Spanish civil war. Orwell joined a Trotskyist group that was affiliated to the Independent Labour Party to whom he then owed allegiance. Known as the POUM (*Partido Obrero de Unificacion Marxista*) it was later suppressed by the Stalin-backed communist party, an experience that scarred Orwell for the rest of his life. Eileen joined him in Spain and narrowly escaped imprisonment when the POUM were suppressed. Orwell was shot through the throat, missing death by a millimetre. He returned to Barcelona only to find that he had escaped death there as well, for POUM militia members were being imprisoned and tortured at will. He and Eileen escaped and returned to their cottage in Wallington, Hertfordshire, remaining there only briefly before his first serious bout of illness since they had been married forced them to go to North Africa for him to recuperate, using a loan from an anonymous sympathiser who admired Orwell's work. Far from being a holiday in the conventional sense Eileen found that Orwell spent much of his time writing articles and other work and on the return trip he spent the daylight hours and late into the evening finishing his novel *Coming Up for Air*. Her life must have required great devotion to Orwell as he struggled against his many difficulties; in the end it was she who saw that the journalism which he much enjoyed doing was wasted time when he could be writing real books. As will become clear it is largely due to her and her lasting vision of the life Orwell, and later their adopted son, should be living that *Nineteen Eighty-Four* came into existence at all.

When they arrived back in England they returned to their Hertfordshire cottage which had been their home since they were first married. But there was to be no peace. Within a short while the war engulfed their rural idyll to which they were never to return.

In the pages that follow the reader will find many echoes of *Nineteen Eighty-Four* from the smallest details through to central themes. The method adopted has been to follow the Orwells' lives from the last peaceful days in Wallington through their time in wartime London to Eileen's tragically early death, and then on to the rest of Orwell's life—he died very shortly after *Nineteen Eighty-Four* was published. Despite Eileen's warnings Orwell had no option but to continue with his journalism and later with work for the BBC throughout the war years. He did almost no creative work and through this period the evolution of the ideas he eventually used in *Nineteen Eighty-Four* are followed as they appear in his journalism. It is interesting that in the majority of cases the ideas in the journalism are simply fragments of the ideas he was developing for his book, rarely the other way around.

There are many books of literary memoirs that describe the war years in London; the two books of Orwell's BBC broadcasts published in 1985 and 1986 give much information of a detailed kind which supplements the material here. Some matters such as '18b', which would have needed no explanation to a contemporary audience, will mean little to a modern reader. Simply put, 18b was the number of the Emergency Powers Regulations, passed when Britain went to war, which enabled people who were thought to have had any association with the enemy to be imprisoned without trial. It was extended, notoriously, by a sub-clause 18b.1a which enabled British citizens to be detained for their political associations, created specifically to enable Sir Oswald Mosley and his followers in the British Union of Fascists to be detained. There is frequent reference to this regulation and Orwell's view of it in the text that follows. If fascists could be detained without trial, so perhaps could Trotskyists if the regime should change.

In the literary world Orwell's own circle included, principally, John Middleton Murry and Max Plowman, the publisher and editor respectively of Orwell's first published work in Britain, sent to them from France; Victor Gollancz who published Orwell's early novels and arranged for him to go to Wigan and see what life was like there, after going down and out in Paris and London; and Fred Warburg, publisher of Orwell's book on Spain *Homage to Catalonia* which Gollancz would not publish, turning it down sight unseen on political grounds.

It is not perhaps necessary to give any detailed account of Orwell's book itself. Its account of a totalitarian Britain set in 1984 (in fact in 1982 as we shall see) in which Winston Smith decides to revolt against the rule of the party by writing a diary to record his own feelings for posterity; Julia's approach to him and their brief affair during which they join a supposedly underground revolutionary movement, The Brotherhood, only to find they have been tricked and betrayed before their revolt has even begun; Winston's torture and subsequent submission to the rule, even the love, of Big Brother the leader; a rough outline of this kind is all that is needed. The reader will find in

9

the following pages repeated references of the kind mentioned before, from details to themes, and the effect is intended to be cumulative. To create separate chapters examing each satiric thrust of *Nineteen Eighty-Four* would be simply to attempt to do Orwell's work over again for him. It has been thought better to follow through the facts of his life and the secret world he and his wife were forced to live in so that we can understand the pressures he was under. Although there seems to be no laughter in *Nineteen Eighty-Four*, perhaps some might just break through when the origin of Syme gabbling on about Newspeak, or the Ministry of Information (MOI) censors rewriting news stories to create 'the truth' are fully understood. There must have been many at the time who saw what he was getting at, people such as Cyril Connolly, but even they would have been chilled by the revelations of what had been happening in the supposed socialist paradise behind the iron curtain. How had Orwell's warning proved so uncannily accurate?

CHAPTER TWO

A Raid in the Country

O rwell's first encounter with the world of *Nineteen Eighty-Four* came just before the outbreak of the Second World War. He was at home in bed in his cottage in the country early one morning when there was a loud knock at the door. He went downstairs wondering who could be calling at that time of day to find himself faced by a group of policemen armed with a search warrant intent on going through the house with a fine-toothed comb. He and Eileen looked on in amazement as they set about their job with zealous enthusiasm. It became clear to Orwell what they were doing when the questions began. One of Orwell's favourite authors was Henry Miller whose books were considered to be pornographic and were banned in Britain. In all innocence Orwell had written off to Miller's publishers in Paris, the Obelisk Press, getting their catalogue and some of Miller's books. It was this letter, intercepted by the authorities, that had lead to the raid.

For the calm of a rural English village to have been invaded in such a brutal way must have been a shock to the local people. The Orwells' lives could never be the same again, especially as they ran the local corner store and most of their daytime customers were local school children. It would have been particularly difficult for Eileen who would inevitably become the centre of gossip. Even today a raid of this kind, though more likely to be made by the social welfare authorities, would shock people and cause scandal. The word to describe this sort of activity now would be the Orwellian 'Big Brother' and there might be some sympathy, but not before the war.

Censorship of the mails was not new in Britain. Although it was considered the hallmark of the European totalitarian bureaucracies in the thirties it had come to Britain earlier in the century at the time of the Boer War. Then the main reason had been to prevent news of the conditions of the concentration camps in South Africa with their appalling death rates becoming public knowledge, to be used by the 'pro-Boers' in efforts to stop the war. The First World War had seen censorship introduced generally on a large scale. In Britain all incoming and outgoing letters were censored. In the extreme cases of letters from soldiers at the front the sheer numbers lead to the introduction of special postcards with standard phrases on them that could be ticked or crossed off to give one of a small number of messages before they went into action. Exactly such cards featured in *Nineteen Eighty-Four*, a throwback rather than a prophecy.

When the war ended the system was wound down except for a small residual presence at the main sorting offices which could respond to requests from the new security services—now called M15—but these were not extensive. There was a lull. Then, at the time of Munich, when war seemed imminent, the system was reintroduced on a full scale though with skeleton staff. Similar steps had been taken in Germany a few years before. Initially the plan had been to stop currency speculation but this soon became cover for a general inspection of the mail. In Britain, clearly, currency control was not available as cover but there was to hand the perfect substitute, the fight against pornography. It was this that Orwell had run foul of. Ten years before and the chances of his letter being intercepted would have been remote. The negative impact of the continental systems of totalitarian Europe were already being felt in this covert reintroduction of full-scale mail censorship. And already planting the seeds of Orwell's final vision of the completely controlled society.

12

Orwell had seen things like this happening in Spain where all mail arrived stamped CENSURA MILITAR. And he knew that things like that were normal in Germany and Russia, but were things getting so bad in Britain? In modern terms a writer who jumped to the conclusion that all his mail was being opened or that he was under some general surveillance would quickly be described as 'paranoid', or a conspiracy theorist, soon to protest that his phone was being tapped. But there was indeed a full-scale censorship system in operation, even if only a selected few were being covered by it. Furthermore Orwell had friends who could soon have told him all about it.

Despite the deep hurt caused by this raid, not least to Eileen, before now the only response of Orwell's that has been recorded was in a few laconic letters that described what had happened and little more. But it seems very likely that he took things further: he was, after all, an ex-policeman himself and knew there would be something more than just the simple facts of the case to produce so drastic a result. His first contact over such matters would have been his publisher at the Adelphi, Middleton Murry. Despite his pacifist views, which Orwell for a time shared, like Orwell he had a more orthodox past. He had been Chief Censor during the First World War. There was nothing about such things he did not know including the latest developments after Munich, for he and others, including a Director of Sotheby's, had been called in to give advice. No doubt he made his new views clear, but the Sotheby man went ahead and built on the structures which had caught Orwell.

There is evidence of a high-level response to Orwell's plight, for he described in a letter to his publisher Gollancz that he had had an apology from a very senior official:

> The police were only carrying out orders and were very nice about it, and even the public prosecutor wrote and said that he understood that as a writer I might have a need for books that it was illegal to possess.

Gollancz would have realised immediately that Orwell had

some special pull, for letters of that kind are rarely written. Orwell clearly had these books which were illegal: only a special intervention could have allayed a prosecution. But there was another quite extraordinary happening involving censorship when war broke out shortly after. Eileen was offered, and took, a job in the Censorship Department. It has been assumed that she had simply had an introduction through one of her university contacts but the job was far too sensitive for that, as we shall see. Sensitive posts, even before the days of moles and molehunts, were not given to people without a check being made. In Eileen's case this would have revealed that her husband was an author who had fought in Spain, that she had been there with him and, even more curious, his books were banned in India. Any one of these facts would have blocked her application unless she had special references. It seems likely that these came from Murry, along with the introduction, perhaps as some recompense for the hurt she had been caused when her house had been raided.

What job was she doing? Orwell's biographers have been vague, surprisingly, since they have remarked that she had an influence in the writing of *Animal Farm*, and censorship is such an important theme in *Nineteen Eighty-Four*. However this silence is explained by the fact that the subject of mail and other censorship systems operated during the war in Britain are still subject to the Official Secrets Act. It was only the accident that the censorship was funded under the Ministry of Information budget during the war, and that some of these papers have inadvertently been released, that enables the facts to be established here. Orwell himself gives us a clue to her work in an entry for his wartime diary for 24 May, 1940:

E[ileen] says the people in the Censorship Department where she works lump all 'red' papers together and look on the *Tribune* [which Orwell wrote for] as being in exactly the same class as the *Daily Worker*. Recently, when the *Daily Worker* and *Action* were prohibited from export, one of her fellow-workers asked her: 'Do you know this paper *The Daily Worker and Action?*'

Orwell's diary was not published during the war; had it been, the censors would have removed this entry. The point of the story as Orwell told it was to illustrate that the staff in the Censorship Department were so politically ignorant that they did not know the difference between the communist paper the *Daily Worker* and that of Sir Oswald Mosley's British Union of Fascists' *Action*. What it tells us is that Eileen was working in one of the most sensitive posts in the censorship system, that issuing the censors' 'stops' which advised those actually doing the censorship what policy they should be following. Material going to America, which Orwell had most contact with, was examined in Liverpool and policy was based on telegrams from the London office, where Eileen worked, written in a combination of slang and cable-ese which strongly resembles that used by O'Brien in *Nineteen Eighty-Four*. The two papers which were 'prohibited from export' as Orwell guardedly put it were banned for a quite specific reason and it is worth describing this in some detail as it helps to place Eileen's department in the scheme of things, and shows also how important for the origins of *Nineteen Eighty-Four* this was.

It had been realised very early on in the war that papers from Britain which reached neutral countries would soon get to Germany and vice-versa. The obvious dangers from a security point of view were blocked by control of the press through a system of 'D' notices which controlled everything that appeared in the British newspapers. But the German radio broadcasters soon found a use for even the most mundane material, weaving it into programmes that had so much local information that people in Britain could not help believing them and spreading them by word of mouth as so-called 'Haw-Haw rumours'. The most serious result, apart from the loss of morale, was a growing belief in the idea of a fifth column in Britain that was supplying this information. For some reason the authorities could not bring themselves to tell the British public what was happening. Instead they resorted to censorship of all papers and, when pressed, suppression of them, first from export, then altogether. The British public believed absolutely in their press and Britain's main morale line was that she was fighting for freedom against the Nazi tyranny. It would have been impossible to explain that the British press was totally censored, even less that it was often used to plant false rumours with the sole intention that these should get back to the Germans. That the British readers believed them too did not matter. This is close to Orwell's world; and Eileen knew it well, for her department not only checked which papers could and which could not go out, but issued the censors' stops which determined what was allowed through from the correspondents of neutral countries actually in Britain.

Eileen's training would have explained to her exactly how the system worked, and one co-ordination section in particular, which she would have known about, has the strongest Orwellian overtones. It was called The Anti-Lie Bureau, and linked some of the most secret facets of postal censorship as well as carrying out its Orwellian task of denying rumours that were reported to it as 'lies', or 'Haw-Haw rumours' which were very often quite true. Eileen's department had the task of going through the papers to discover possible sources for the various rumours circulating. When the incidence of comment on Nazi radio from a particular paper reached an intolerable point, one assumes, then comment would be made and finally an outright ban from export followed.

The Anti-Lie Bureau also acted as a co-ordination centre for the circulation of certain letters which had been intercepted in transit and which were actually shown to those who were said to have a 'need to know'. Orwell was one of a group of people at the BBC who knew about this as we shall see in chapter five. That he was referring directly to it in *Nineteen Eighty-Four* is obvious. Winston

16

Smith, wondering how he is to get in touch with Julia says:

As for sending a letter through the mails, it was out of the question. By a routine that was not even secret all letters were opened in transit.

It is difficult now to realise the extent of publicly known mail censorship that went on and was accepted as normal. Each letter entering or leaving the country was opened and examined without any exception, tens of millions a month, and resealed with a printed label giving the number of the censor who had opened it in case there was any query. In extreme cases where blue pencil or physical removal by scissors was not enough the entire letter was returned, again with a label on the front saying this had been done. The effect on someone receiving such a letter back from their local postman can be imagined, although perhaps not quite as bad as the shock the Orwells had when their home was raided in the early hours of the morning.

The public knew this was going on and approved of it, and it might seem unnecessary for Orwell to incorporate a warning against censorship in *Nineteen Eighty-Four*. However the process of censorship was not as benign as the public thought. When letters were opened their contents were not simply cancelled if any censors stops were broken. Anything of the slightest interest on a wide range of subjects from economics to morale was taken down and reported on special forms (illustrated here). These forms were sent to the office in London where Eileen Orwell worked. There all the information in them was collated and recorded by a department called Information and Records, the acronym IRD being commonly used, or the office slang 'Rec.Dep' used in *Nineteen Eighty-Four*. This meant that a very high proportion of people who wrote abroad had their comments on file in the Censorship Department.

The IRD did not stop at building up a profile of people based on the contents of their mail. Any information relating to internal security matters was handed over to MI5—many examples of these forms have been seen with the circulation box marked MI5 so there can be no doubt about this. MI5 were thus able to build up their files on the individuals and organisations concerned. If they had a name they wanted information on they could similarly access the information held on the censors' files at the MOI. We can already see the Orwellian nightmare emerging from the fog of lies that has concealed this kind of activity over the years. A senior official several rungs above Eileen in the Censorship Department at one point attempted to resign from his post saying that if it were ever discovered what they were doing they would be called the British Gestapo. Things were not quite that bad—there was no torture, no 'Room 101' in the MOI—but as far as surveillance went it was as thorough as could be imagined.

Orwell's comment about mail being opened would have been seen by the general reader as, perhaps, an intellectual complaining about something that could readily be explained by the war and the needs of the emergency. But they would not have known of the thoroughness of the surveillance, or of one other dimension which the Orwells knew about: internal censorship. This differed from overseas censorship in being avowedly secret. No labels were used, and instructions have survived giving officers detailed guidance on how to ensure that letters removed from the mails should be kept with their envelopes at all times so that they could be replaced and sent on. Only if the envelope was lost or damaged would a decison have to be taken on whether to destroy the letter, or attach a normal sticker leaving the recipient to imagine the letter had gone through the foreign mail system by mistake.

The internal mail censorship seems to have developed on a piecemeal basis. Initially 'spot checks' of mail posted near air force bases were called for to ensure that no letters had been sent by men going on raids wishing to evade the usual forces censorship for domestic reasons. The problem with this action was that ordinary mail was being opened on a large scale in these exercises and often material would come to light which seemed to require action. This was particularly the case with evidence of infringement of the wartime emergency regulations, rationing being the most common, and for straightforward criminal activity. It was decided that information in these letters and, again, the letters themselves could be shown to those with a 'need to know'. One well-known case concerned some rationing coupons which were being sent illegally through the post. They were intercepted and sent to the Ministry of Food who prosecuted those involved. The ministry officials forgot to give themselves a cover story to explain how they got their information and this mistake came to light at the trial which led to the case being raised by an MP and to a general suspicion that civilian mails within Britain were in some way being looked at. The full facts were not discovered by the MP, or the press. Even if they had been nothing could have been published about it.

Orwell's off-hand comment that 'by a routine that was not even secret all letters were opened in transit' has appeared, no doubt, as an invention of a dying, slightly paranoid man. But it is a simple extension of what was happening to all overseas mail—quite openly—to what he knew through Eileen, and later his own knowledge, was happening to internal mails also. Those at whom his satires were aimed would have known quite well where this shaft was directed. Also Winston and Julia in *Nineteen Eighty-Four* were party members, numbered in their thousands rather than the millions of the proles, the ordinary people whose activities did not matter. Far from being a futuristic fantasy this level of surveillance was well within the capabilities of MI5 and the MOI at the time Orwell conceived his satire in 1943. It is the sort of exercise that can be carried out today with the greatest of ease in Britain, although not perhaps on the scale of that carried on by the Stasi in East Germany: there is no party. Who knows but that, if Orwell's warning had not been heeded, in Britain there would have been one also.

The sequel to that early morning call on a small village

shop in rural Hertfordshire can hardly have been imagined by any writer, let alone one who based his work on reality as much as Orwell. But the first hint of the nightmare facing him and countless thousands of others was there in the knock on the door, the ring of stern faces, always exceptionally polite but with questions that had to be answered. The totalitarian bureaucracy of a Europe about to be plunged into war had reached England, and it was not to pass the Orwells by. That it was his wife who first took the brunt of the shock of this totalitarianism must have annoyed him the more. Their lives would never be the same, but he could at least speak out about it. For the moment he was not sure how, and whilst Eileen went off to her work in the Censorship Department during the weeks that followed the outbreak of war he remained in his cottage.

CHAPTER THREE

Peace and War

After Eileen was plunged into the embryo world of Big Brother and censorship she rarely came back down to the cottage which no doubt felt differently to her since the raid. Orwell stayed behind, seeming not much different from other intellectuals who went to ground for the duration of the hostilities, or even escaped to America. In reality he was a very lonely man. He had taken an almost unique stand on the justness of the war which had alienated him from those closest to him in the years before the war, but without finding another role for himself. The key to this change was his revulsion against the world of pacifism and pacifists in which his first editor Max Plowman and Middleton Murry were leading figures. Orwell had written a pacifist pamphlet and toyed with closer connection to the Peace Pledge Union to which many of his friends belonged. His conversion to support for the war he described in very personal terms:

> The night before the Russo-German pact was announced I dreamed that the war had started. It was one of those dreams which, whatever Freudian meaning they may have, do sometimes reveal to you the real state of your feelings. It taught me two things, first that I should be simply relieved when the long-dreaded war started, and secondly, that I was patriotic at heart, would not sabotage or act against my own side, would support the war, would fight in it if possible.

21

I came downstairs to find the newspaper announcing Ribbentrop's flight to Moscow. So war was coming, and the government, even the Chamberlain government, was assured of my loyalty.

Such dreams feature in *Nineteen Eighty-Four*, and the relief at war starting has itself a hint of the party edict, 'WAR IS PEACE'. When he came downstairs and found his newspaper the effect on his life was as great as when he came down the same stairs to find the police waiting to search his house. That day he went to visit the novelist L. H. Myers at his home with other guests including, it appears, Max Plowman. Whatever they talked of Orwell must have made his conversion known, for he never spoke to Plowman again. When Plowman died in 1941 Orwell wrote an absolutely typical letter of condolence to his widow:

I had not seen him for nearly two years, I deeply disagreed with him over the issue of pacifism, but though I am sorry about that you will perhaps understand when I say that I feel at bottom it didn't matter.

Orwell's renunciation of all that Plowman stood for must have been keenly felt, particularly as it was Plowman who had arranged for Orwell and his wife to go to North Africa using money that had come from Myers, a fact Orwell was unaware of when he visited his home for the week before the war. It must have been a delicate occasion. Orwell was there when war broke out and recorded in his war diary for 27 June the following year that Myers had made very accurate predictions of the way the war would go on that very day: 'He said nothing would happen all winter, Italy would be treated with great respect and then suddenly come in against us, and the German aim would be to force on England a puppet government through which Hitler could rule England without the mass of the people grasping what was happening'.

Orwell's argument with the pacifists who held such views

was that they were playing into the hands of the dictators, to use a phrase he later came to hate. And his view was rapidly proved correct in a series of astonishing broadcasts by Middleton Murry on the BBC which took the pacifist line to just such extremes. The broadcasts were greeted with outrage, and it can hardly be wondered that questions were asked in the House of Commons about talks which included passages with such outright, even adoring, praise for the leader of a country with which we were at war:

> Hitler is the unique creation, the prophetic spirit [of the coming world totalitarianism] of the civilisation to which we belong. He is the prince of this world—the man who served his apprenticeship to life in the doss-houses of a great European capital and drew his grim conclusions. It is time we drew ours. It was done for us years ago by William Blake:
>
> "Man must and will have some religion: if he has not the religion of Jesus, he will have the religion of Satan and will erect the synagogue of Satan, calling the prince of this world God and destroying all who do not worship Satan under the name God."

The German pacifist black propaganda stations, purporting to be in Britain, but actually broadcast from the continent, could not have done it better. And in fact, as the Nazi-Soviet pact was in full action at this time, and the BBC had within it some of the most expert Soviet moles, notably Guy Burgess, it is quite possible that these talks were deliberately planted. Reading them now (they were published as *The Christian News-Letter Books No.2 Europe in Travail* with the preface dated 1 January, 1940) it is difficult to see what could have been in the censor's mind when he passed them. Orwell, for his part, can only have seen confirmation of everything he thought about Murry, Plowman and those around them. The religious element in *Nineteen Eighty-Four* with the woman gesturing towards the giant image of Big Brother and uttering the words 'My saviour' has the strongest echoes of Blake's warning, with Middleton Murry

23

going further still and putting Hitler forward as the prince of this world, to be worshipped as Satan under the name God.

This defeatist strain developed rapidly during the phoney war and did not subside when Hitler's forces began to pour over Europe. Indeed the world famous pacifist leader Gandhi advised the British to submit peaceably to the inevitability of Hitler's conquest of Britain and simply resist passively when the opportunity arose. Orwell hated this kind of talk as much as if he had never left the Indian Imperial Police, and his view of Gandhi would have been regarded as strictly orthodox, even by their stern standards. But, much as he wanted to get involved in the war, he found that he could not. His health was appalling. His political record was particularly difficult also because this not only stopped him getting into uniform, but from getting accepted into any other post. However great his hatred of the Nazi-Soviet pact it must have grown still stronger as he realised that despite being on the 'wrong' side in Spain, fighting with the POUM, the Trotskyist militia, he was still on the 'wrong' side after the declaration of the Nazi-Soviet pact because the officials in Britain could not follow that all those who fought for the Republic in Spain were not necessarily fervent admirers of Stalin. Indeed the irony of the fact that, after calling the POUM objectively pro-fascist and accusing them of acting secretly in league with Franco, it was *they*, the Soviets, who finally collaborated was completely lost on these officials.

All Orwell's attempts at finding 'war work' failed and he was obliged to retreat once again to his cottage and spend his time digging in a bumper crop of potatoes against the rationing which he was sure would come. The persona of the writer as an isolated person, the origin of Orwell's image of him as *The Last Man*, which gave *Nineteen Eighty-Four* its first title, undoubtedly took shape here. Although he saw few people he wrote letters and some of these reveal the genesis of what was to become his last book. Writing to Geoffrey Gorer, a man he had met through his books, always the most welcome friendship an author can have, he talked of his plans for a book:

I've now got an idea for a really big novel, I mean big in bulk
and I want to lie fallow before doing it. Of course God knows
what hope there is of making a living out of writing in the
future or where we'll all be in a few years hence.

Earlier he had said he was incubating an enormous novel, 'the
family saga sort of thing', but there was here an element of
frustration at his situation which was making the idea of any
kind of family life impossible. Eileen was working ten hours a
day at her job and could only be home every other weekend, if
that. For the rest of the time she was staying with her brother
and sister-in-law in Greenwich. Orwell made occasional visits
and they spent Christmas there as it was impossible for them
to spend it in the country. There was a further period of weeks
at this home-from-home when he had a recurrence of illness,
a foreshadowing of the disease which was to kill him. His
letters began to show he was missing his normal life with
Eileen. He wrote to Gorer that she was being worked to
death in 'her office'—he could not name it because of the
Official Secrets Act—adding 'besides making it impossible for
us to be together'. He even began ending his letters with some
phrase such as 'Eileen would send her love if she were here'.

It must have been obvious to Orwell that a move was
inevitable and that the pre-war country idyll would have to
end. He wrote in his diary of killing the chickens and other
animals where before he had thought that he might increase
them, and even breed rabbits to become self-sufficient. Money
was at bottom the problem, for he ought really to have been able
to get a flat in London for him and Eileen to live in. He again set
about trying to get a place on a training course to do machine
draughtsmanship, which he could have coped with as he did
much amateur work on a lathe. But he also started writing more
essays and doing reviews. This proved the way forward, but it
meant that his idea of a book on the great scale had to go by
the board and his creative work ceased. From this time until he
left the BBC the development of the ideas that produced *Animal*

25

Farm and *Nineteen Eighty-Four* have to be followed through his other writings. One of the first books he reviewed during 1940 illustrates exactly what was happening.

Orwell's review of Hitler's *Mein Kampf* is a very unusual piece of writing and has been ignored by critics, no doubt because of the quite extraordinary statements about Hitler in it. In fact what he wrote reflects strongly the ideas of Middleton Murry, and is of similar interest for a study of *Nineteen Eighty-Four* and leader-worship. The key passage, which must have shocked many of his friends, seemed to be praise of Hitler.

> I should like to put it on record that I have never been able to dislike Hitler . . . The fact is that there is something deeply appealing about him. One feels it again when one sees his photographs . . . It is a pathetic, dog-like face, the face of a man suffering under intolerable wrongs. In a rather more manly way it reproduces the expression of innumerable pictures of Christ crucified, and there is little doubt that that is how Hitler sees himself . . . He is the martyr, the victim. Prometheus chained to the rock, the self-sacrificing hero who fights single handed against impossible odds. One feels, as with Napoleon, that he is fighting against destiny, that he *can't* win, and yet that he somehow deserves to.

It is true he did qualify his remarks by saying that if he ever got within reach of Hitler he would certainly kill him, but that he could feel no personal animosity when doing so. Later scholars and readers who have come across this passage have no doubt shuddered and moved on, unaware of the context of the remarks, or of the influence of Murry and the Christian pacifist movement which Orwell had been so close to. Orwell admits that he is attracted to the photographic image of Hitler, and the man himself, and it is clear that Middleton Murry also saw Hitler in some such way; but Orwell is quite certain that Hitler, like Stalin, was a force for evil and would have to be done away with if at all possible. The 'phoney war' saw this kind of development, even the publication of *Mein Kampf* was a sign of it. Middleton Murry clearly stated that totalitarianism was here to stay; Orwell could never accept this in any form.

The identification of Hitler with Christ, or in Murry's terms the Devil as Christ, is to modern eyes the most puzzling. This identification was *literally* made at the time and Orwell commented on a group that announced after the war that Hitler had been Christ re-incarnated; he may have known that there was a group during the war that said the same thing. Psychologically this is the underlying totalitarian principle in *Nineteen Eighty-Four* with worship of Big Brother replacing that of Christ. Indeed as Orwell pointed out frequently those on the far left in Britain did unwittingly transfer the legacy of their theological tradition onto Stalin without realising what they were doing; they worshipped power. In the case of 'Stalin's Englishmen' they were prepared to betray their country for his cause just as religious zealots did in the sixteenth century, happily going to the stake with the sacred name on their lips. The vanity of the twentieth century was that it thought it had got beyond this kind of thing. In another prescient review of a book, *The Thirties*, Orwell made valid points about the author, Malcolm Muggeridge, who wrestled to the end of his life with just these problems of Christianity in the modern world.

Talking of what had happened in the thirties he remarked that it was as if human types which could only be read about in history books had suddenly reappeared in the world, like the Spanish inquisitors. The reforms and advances of the nineteenth and twentieth centuries had not been enough to ensure happiness for mankind:

By themselves they lead merely to the nightmare we are now enduring: endless war and endless underfeeding for the sake of war, slave populations toiling behind barbed wire, women dragged shrieking to the block, cork-lined cellars where the executioner blows your brains out . . . we can be pretty certain what is ahead of us. Wars and yet more wars, revolutions and counter-revolutions, Hitlers and

27

Super-Hitlers—and so downward into abysses which are too horrible to contemplate . . .

However no one was able to suggest a remedy to avoid these catastrophes. Mentioning one of the key books of the twentieth century, Hilaire Belloc's *The Servile State*, which foretold either a world of slave states, which we have barely escaped today, or a return to small-holdings of the kind Orwell was trying to make survive at Wallington and would later try again on Jura, Orwell could see no answer in practical terms there either. He went on to suggest the one solution which Murry and the others actually professed: universal brotherhood, the original Christian doctrine of the brotherhood of man. In what was probably one of his last uses of the word in its original sense before it was reborn in *Nineteen Eighty-Four*, Orwell points to one of the problems of *that* idea:

> Brotherhood implies a common father. Therefore it is often argued that men can never develop the sense of community unless they believe in God. The answer is that in a half-conscious way most of them have developed it already. Man is not an individual he is only a cell in an everlasting body, and he is simply unaware of it. There is no other way of explaining why it is that men will die in battle.

He went on to talk of Aldous Huxley's *Brave New World* as being a good caricature of 'the hedonistic Utopia':

> . . . the kind of things [the hedonistic Utopia] that seemed possible and even imminent before Hitler appeared, but had no relation to the actual future. What we are moving towards at this moment is something more like the Spanish Inquisition, and probably far worse, thanks to the radio and the secret police. There is little chance of escaping it unless we can reinstate the belief in human brotherhood without the need of a 'next world' to give it meaning.

It is rare for a writer's thoughts to be so clearly traceable in the process of evolution as they are here. In the months to come

Orwell was driven far away from the idea of brotherhood, so far that it became a key element in *Nineteen Eighty-Four* with the leader modelled on Hitler, Stalin or even Gandhi transformed into Big Brother. There is no trace in his letters or writing that the idea for *Nineteen Eighty-Four* had appeared at this time; the novel he was contemplating was still the large Victorian family saga perhaps put into his mind by the extensive essay he wrote on Dickens. In any event there was no possibility of his staying in Wallington whilst the ideas developed.

Orwell was not alone in his predicament and by 1940 a number of new literary ventures had begun to appear, with some revival of the fortunes of the publishers. The expected universal bombing had not occurred and to publishers' surprise and delight people tended to read a lot more when they went down to the shelters. In one of the few pieces of good fortune to come to Orwell at this time an old school friend of his, with him both at prep school and Eton, Cyril Conolly, was one of those who had decided to start a new magazine called *Horizon*. It was to become the most important literary periodical of wartime London and opened a new door for Orwell who contributed to it almost immediately, publishing his famous essay on 'Boys Weeklies' there. At the same time he began writing for the magazine *Tribune* which is still thriving today. Its present position on the far left of the Labour party has misled people into projecting this identity onto the paper Orwell wrote for, there was even the phrase 'Tribune socialist' used at the time, and later, but with differing meanings as we shall see in chapter ten. As a final string to his journalistic bow Orwell began doing theatre and film criticism for *Time and Tide* whose political affiliation Orwell aptly summed up in his cryptic remark '*Time and Tide* writes for no man'. Together these factors made a move to London not only probable but likely—editors *will* deal with people in the country, particularly nowadays with the fax in every literary home, but then they preferred people to be on the spot. Besides journalism, Orwell seems to have made fresh contact with the publisher Fred Warburg and set a number of projects afoot which will be mentioned in the next chapter. All of them meant he had to be in London and although some did not materialise others did, the most important of them being *The Lion and the Unicorn: Socialism and the English Genius*.

There was one other essay written at Wallington which foreshadowed a major theme of *Nineteen Eighty-Four*, that of the corruption of the English language, the arrival of synthetic languages such as Esperanto and the simplified Basic English which he ruthlessly satirised as Newspeak. The essay was called 'New Words'. In *Nineteen Eighty-Four* Syme speaks lovingly of the destruction of words. In 1940 Orwell made a very good case for the increase of words, and the failings of the language under the impact of modern developments. Nowadays that is a commonplace and words are invented and recorded every year in large numbers. In Orwell's day people were hardly conscious of this and his essay begins with the ludicrous suggestion that 'English gains about six and looses about four words a year'. This cannot have been true at the time of course, but Orwell clearly believed it and went on to talk about the creation of several thousand new words:

> The solution I suggest is to invent new words as deliberately as we would invent new parts for a motor car engine.

There are echoes here of *Nineteen Eighty-Four* and machines for writing poetry but, like 'brotherhood', the idea has been turned on its head. It would take three years in the tortured world of wartime London before his ideas became clear enough for them to develop into a more lasting form than journalism.

CHAPTER FOUR

Wartime London

Living in London during the Second World War meant living through the blitz, either the threat of destruction, or the bombs themselves falling sometimes as high explosive bombs, or later the pilotless jet-propelled bombs, the V1s, or the rocket bombs, the V2s. The Orwells experienced them all and moved four times during their days in London at least twice because of raids, although luckily neither was hurt.

Their first flat was in a mews off Baker Street, well known amongst a select circle as being the mews where the first Bentley motor car was constructed. They lived in an old-fashioned block of flats called Dorset Chambers built before running water and other facilities were considered essential. Their stay was brief, a bomb fell just along from them and the damage was warning enough of what would happen to their home if a bomb fell any closer. Instead they moved to a block of flats on the other side of the park which is quite obviously the original of Victory mansions in *Nineteen Eighty-Four*. Not only is its physical location the same, from its roof the tower of the Ministry of Information (as it then was) is clearly visible rising above the Georgian buildings which surround it. It has itself been dwarfed by other skyscrapers but was in its time the tallest building in London. When Orwell looked across London at it, no doubt Eileen explained what really went on there. Orwell looking out at the Ministry of Information became Winston Smith looking at the Ministry of Truth.

The reason for living in this modern tower, which Orwell did not find congenial, was that, as he says of the tower of the Ministry of Truth, bombs could not damage it. This was literally true: the author was living in an adjacent block to Orwell's at the time which suffered a direct hit by a high explosive bomb during a raid. It was possible to walk along to the section which had been hit and see open space with water from fractured mains pouring down through the blackness, and then return to a flat in another part of the block which had remained entirely undamaged. There is a well known account of Orwell at dinner in a friend's flat in a modern block when a bomb fell opposite. Orwell remarked that if they had been in an ordinary working man's house at street level they would all have been as dead as mutton, and this has later been taken as his typical inverted class consciousness. In fact it was the cold realism of someone who had fought in a war. Orwell's real feelings for Victory Mansions and of what it was like living there, can be seen from his graphic descriptions of it in *Nineteen Eighty-Four*.

The opening sequence of *Nineteen Eighty-Four* in Winston Smith's flat is the closest Orwell gets to self parody, perhaps even unintentionally. Winston has come to the flat to start a diary, and the first thing he can think of writing in it is an account of a visit to 'the flicks' the night before. There were two reasons which brought Orwell to London. First the need to see the films for *Time and Tide*, his journalism, and secondly, and a little more mysteriously, to write a diary. Orwell began to write this diary as soon as he came to London, seemingly with a view to its being published from the first. Initially these wartime diaries suffered the fate of a number of his writings at this time and were rejected. Their very conception seems unclear. It is known that they were originally intended to be published jointly with a diary of a similar kind written by Inez Holden, whom Orwell had met through their mutual publisher Fred Warburg. Such a project would be uncommon now, and then was almost unheard of, and yet the facts have been repeated in one book after another without comment. We shall look in chapter sixteen at the friendship between Orwell and Inez Holden, but for the moment the point is that Orwell seems to have started work on the book as soon as he got to London and therefore to have had a contract for it before he moved. In a pattern which was often repeated, and will be seen again at the time of his move to Jura, Orwell arranged some major project to cover the costs of his moves. The diary contained references to his going to the cinema, just as Winston Smith's does, though with the same fictional transformation of circumstances as with Victory Mansions.

Apart from his visits to the 'flicks' Orwell's life in London revolved around the new political and social groups who replaced the pacifists he had deserted. Eileen was now with him again but was crushed for some eighteen months by the death of her brother at Dunkirk. She did not shun society but was simply very withdrawn. Tosco Fyvel, who worked with Orwell at this time editing a series called Searchlight Books, probably another part of the deal he had made with Warburg before coming to London, has left a memorable and moving description of her:

> Eileen accompanied him on his visits to us, but we all noticed a profound change in her. She seemed to sit in the garden sunk in unmoving silence while we talked. Mary [Fyvel] . . . observed that Eileen not only looked tired and drawn but was drably and untidily dressed. Trying in vain to involve Eileen in conversation Mary said that she seemed to have become completely withdrawn. Since Orwell and Eileen were reticent to a degree, it was only after her second or third visit that we learned that her brother Laurence had been killed.

They also sometimes went to the Cafe Royal, another centre of literary life, dominated by Cyril Connolly, Kingsley Martin, the editor of the *New Statesman*, and others including Stephen

Spender. Orwell couldn't stand what he called 'that Cafe Royal set' and, if the Chestnut Tree Cafe in *Nineteen Eighty-Four* is modelled on it as it seems to be, then Winston's recollection of being there without any clear memory of how he happened to find himself there would be about right. Inez Holden once took the Orwells to it to meet Anthony Powell; on another occasion there was a fierce argument between Orwell and Stephen Spender on the reason for Spender's going to Spain and his role there, when Orwell had fought and only escaped death by a hair's-breadth.

The reason for attending the 'salon' at the Cafe Royal for many people was to keep in the swim, and, in real terms, ensure a steady flow of commissions for articles in the magazines run by Connolly, Martin and the others was maintained. In Orwell's case he was only partially dependent on them since he had previously ensured his position through Warburg, but he did write pieces and one for the *New Statesman*, an essay on Jack London's *The Iron Heel*, which had been recently republished, seems definitely to have influenced Orwell and the background thoughts about his next book. These were developing slowly, although, as he said to many correspondents, he was doing no actual work on it. The title of his review 'Prophesies of Fascism' could indeed be taken as the theme of *Nineteen Eighty-Four* as Orwell expressly stated it, a warning of what might happen if there was not great vigilance. After discussing the shortcomings of Jack London's book in literary terms he goes on to point out that London realised what Wells and Huxley did not—that a hedonistic society would not survive and that the new order would be tough and spartan. However he went on to mention another book, Ernest Bramah's *The Secret of The League*, published in 1907:

> The author imagines a Labour Government coming into office with so huge a majority that it is impossible to dislodge them. They do not, however, introduce a full socialist economy. They merely continue to operate capitalism for

their own benefit by constantly raising wages, creating a huge army of bureaucrats and taxing the upper classes out of existence.

Here was indeed a warning that parallels the kind of warning given in *Nineteen Eighty-Four*, and, in fact, a very good prediction of the actual actions of the post-war Labour Governments. In the final chapters we will examine the extent to which Orwell's fears of a communist takeover of the Labour Party, rather than Bramah's mild hypothesis, influenced *Nineteen Eighty-Four*

A key element in Jack London's *Iron Heel* is that (as we have mentioned in the first chapter) he represents an *American* voice and an American perspective which also begins to emerge in one of Orwell's most interesting books written at this time, *The Lion and the Unicorn*. Towards the end of the book Orwell begins to talk of the English-speaking culture. Saying that Britain should look to America as her natural ally, he goes on to talk about the role of the English-speaking peoples as the bulwark against fascism and totalitarianism. In words used earlier but worth repeating:

> The whole English-speaking world is haunted by the idea of human equality, and though it would be simply a lie to say that either we or the Americans have ever acted up to our professions, still, the *idea* is there, and it is capable of one day becoming a reality. From the English-speaking culture if it does not perish, a society of free and equal human beings will ultimately arise.

And here also he for the first time envisages clearly a situation where Britain would be part of 'Oceania', and not 'Eurasia' which is Europe with parts of Asia, i.e. Russia.

The movement in his thinking from the near-pacifism of the pre-war thought of his older friends was considerable, and *The Lion and the Unicorn* is a personal manifesto in a real sense. It was to be set against the continuous outpouring of

35

pacifist sentiment that his former friends were putting out, despite the emergency powers regulations which prohibited spreading alarm and despondency. Middleton Murry was again in the forefront in this activity and he wrote a key text in a series of pamphlets put out by the Peace Pledge Union under the general title *The Bond of Peace*. Murry's was called *The Brotherhood of Peace* and carried the idea of the Christian brotherhood a shade further, almost to the point at which it becomes recognisable in terms of *Nineteen Eighty-Four*:

> The fraternity of pacifists must be prepared to work in the interstices of a virtual totalitarianism until life becomes human again.

Here is the brotherhood to which Winston and Julia are attracted, and the background of their existence is also similar:

> There may conceivably be a long period—let us hope there is—when the nations will be in a state of war, because there is no other condition for them to be in while they remain what they are, and yet will really refrain from waging war, except on a relatively insignificant scale. Enough fantastic things have happened for that to be not wholly inconceivable. If it were so we should be grateful: but our particular business would be no less urgent then before—to spread among men, by precept and example, a sense of the necessity of a fundamentally different way of life: indeed of taking control of their own lives from the clutches of the impersonal forces that now govern them.

This response to the totalitarian world of Britain at war against totalitarianism is almost exactly the condition of Winston in *Nineteen Eighty-Four*, yet Orwell here saw that the result of this attitude would be, inevitably, a collapse of morale which would lead to a successful invasion should Hitler have decided to undertake it. Murry's thought is at times difficult to follow—he was clearly writing under extreme pressure both personal and political. The logic of his position was a retreat from the world which he finally carried out by setting up a communal farm. Orwell must have been only too aware that many of his own ideas (his Scottish island, his ideas of a self-sufficient community) were not very different from Murry's. And perhaps he was not himself sure how to argue his way out of that particular position at first, only knowing that he had realised, after his dream, that he was totally opposed to all such activity in a war. It was nothing more than a betrayal of one's country. That he should give Winston and Julia similar aims, at least in general outline, is a measure of his own initial attraction. The satire comes later, in the first drafts of *Nineteen Eighty-Four* when Orwell has the Christian pacifists demanding that people in their tens of thousands be buried alive in retaliation for some atrocity of the other side. The exact argument between Orwell and Murry as it developed over the next few years will be looked at in later chapters. Here it is sufficient to realise that it was amongst these people, initially, that Orwell saw the dangers he wanted to warn against.

The diary that Orwell kept through this period only survives in the version edited for publication, but it is still of great significance. His interest in America, and insight into the importance of America for the outcome of the war was acute:

> This morning's papers make it reasonably clear, at any rate until after the presidential election, the USA will not do anything, i.e. will not declare war, which in fact is what matters. For if the USA is not actually in the war, there will never be sufficient control of either business or labour to speed up production of armaments. In the last war this was the case even when the USA was a belligerent.

He was also very well aware of the fact that if America also succumbed to the totalitarian wave then there would be nothing left but to die fighting, adding 'but one must

37

above all die *fighting* and have the satisfaction of killing somebody else first'. This kind of remark put Orwell beyond the pale with many of his friends in the pacifist movement, and many on the left generally. Indeed those who started talking about his background and a 'reversion to type'—the Imperial policeman—could find evidence to support that view in much of his thinking, although there were still many signs of his typical off-beat humour and viewpoint. The American perspective would have seemed a sure sign to left-wing colleagues that he was drifting far off to the right, and the absence of any significant left movement in America in recent times has lead to an exaggeration of this idea, although at the time there were many communists in America, and Orwell could report in his diary that American communists were working with local Nazis to prevent American arms reaching Britain. This kind of perspective does not exist now but again Orwell had recently re-read Jack London's book and saw America in a quite different light. Perhaps for this reason he took up an offer to write a regular newsletter for the left-wing magazine *Partisan Review*. Its politics were congenial to him—anti-Stalinist—and his contributions were valued greatly. They are still interesting today as historical documents.

Writing for a magazine published overseas in wartime was not something that could be done haphazardly, as if there were no war on, even if America was neutral and a strong potential ally soon to become an ally in good earnest. The censorship operated most zealously in such cases and Orwell had his first serious contact with the system that Eileen had lived with, on the inside, over his contributions to these magazines. He had suggested in one letter that any German parachutist who landed in Britain might find himself being lynched. The censors removed this although when the text arrived in New York there was no trace of the removal. The entire sheet had been retyped. From the description we have given of Eileen's department it can easily be seen how this could be done. Every essay or letter of interest had its contents typed out for their routine reports, so that typing out an amended sheet would pose no problems. For those who did not know the kind of detailed report that the censors regularly made it could hardly be imagined that such a thing could happen. Orwell had to write specifically to his American editors to explain, although the censors were very adept at intercepting follow-up letters of this kind. A serious example of a security leak at the BBC revealed this clearly: a woman had had a letter opened by the censor and had mentioned this to a colleague at the BBC. By complete chance he had already seen this letter or 'intercept' and was foolish enough to say so. The letter referred to BBC programmes and hence was deemed proper to be circulated to the BBC. His friend wrote a full account of this to her correspondent without realising that that letter too would arrive immediately in her MOI file right next to the first letter. This was what happened and the BBC official was seriously reprimanded. The world of *Nineteen Eighty-Four* was very much alive then.

The existence of left-wing thought in America, and Orwell's direct relationship to it, both at its roots as found in Jack London and in such figures as Austin Lewis, explains his continuing attachment to socialism which many later figures on the left have found hard to believe. In Orwell's book *The Lion and the Unicorn* he still draws a great distinction between fascism and the practices of European totalitarian states, and British and American traditions of freedom:

> The whole conception of the militarised continental state with its secret police, its censored literature and its conscript labour, is utterly different from that of the loose maritime democracy . . .

What Orwell could not have imagined is that all these elements would come to pass in Britain within a few years, and that, although he was not about to become conscripted labour, he would find his books being censored completely—not just the odd phrase—and find himself a subject of interest to the security services.

Within a very short space of time Orwell had settled into wartime London life, 'landing on his feet' as all Etonians are said to do no matter what the circumstances. But he cannot have been happy with the fact that there was an unmistakable air of corruption around most of the people he found himself working with. Although he stuck by Cyril Connolly he came to hate Kingsley Martin, and the fellow-travellers who he so brilliantly satirises in *Nineteen Eighty-Four* as the failed revolutionaries brought back briefly from the dead in the Chestnut Tree Cafe. As an intellectual he would have been almost friendless had it not been for the circle around Warburg, Tosco Fyvel, Inez Holden and others he met less regularly. And he was clear also that his overview of what was really happening that he sent to America was valid: there would have been few who could have seen things validly from a New York standpoint, writing a regular column from London for New York, who was not simply someone who was about to get on to a ship and go there, as so many intellectuals did. Orwell could see the way things were and wanted to stay and fight to protect what he believed in.

Although Orwell despised the pacifists for what they believed in he knew that they did not have an easy time of it. Just as there was a difference between going to Spain as a fellow-travelling intellectual and actually fighting, perhaps being killed, so also, paradoxically, there was a similar difference between being a left-wing intellectual who somehow fiddled his way out of the war and stayed in London, and being a pacifist who had to face rigorous pressure from the authorities. Orwell's transformation of the idea of the brotherhood movement from what it was in Murry's thought at this time into something far more sinister is complex and reflects in its turn development of Middleton Murry's idea at the time of the dropping of the first atomic bombs, as we shall see. There were also, however, strong links with the harsher reality of political fighting in 1940 and 1941. These happenings affected Orwell's life profoundly, for he did not simply reject brotherhood, pacifism and fellow-travelling: he fought a war against it and was never forgiven for doing so. Having looked briefly at the cosy world of the Cafe Royal and the *bon viveur* socialists, the 'Bollinger Bolsheviks' as they were later called, it is now necessary to look at the darker side of dissent, and come to terms with the fact that Orwell was on the side of the oppressors not the oppressed as far as his erstwhile friends were concerned, just as O'Brien, at first Winston's friend, becomes his persecutor.

CHAPTER FIVE

The Tribunal

W hen Parsons, the most servile member of the party in *Nineteen Eighty-Four*, is accused of thoughtcrime and thrown into the cellars of the Ministry of Love to be tortured and broken, he says to Winston Smith:

> Between you and me, old man, I'm glad they got me before it went any further. Do you know what I am going to say to them when I go up before the tribunal? 'Thank you'. I'm going to say, 'Thank you for saving me before it was too late'.

There is no other reference to this tribunal in the book, and today, particularly for audiences in America and around the world it is difficult to know what might be meant. When Orwell wrote his book the word 'tribunal' still had a uniquely chilling effect on those who had decided during the war that they wanted to be conscientious objectors, or those who were threatened with detention under 18b, or later those who wanted to change their jobs but were forbidden to do so without 'good reason'. These tribunals continued after the war as a central element in the system of bureaucratic totalitarianism which ran Britain in its darkest days and has survived in a modified and often more benevolent form right up to the present day. It grew up, hardly noticed, as a useful and far more efficient alternative to the jury system where the twelve people randomly chosen had an annoying tendency to express the common wisdom and not deliver the required opinion, even on the plainest evidence, if they felt something was wrong.

Orwell would have been well acquainted with both the conscientious objectors' tribunals, and those set up as an alleged safeguard against random detention without trial under regulation 18b. No doubt the words 'tribunal' and 'detention' were never uttered in the Cafe Royal but they were there in people's minds.

The existence of conscientious objectors, and of procedures to allow them to avoid call-up and actual fighting was a tribute to the freedom which existed in Britain and had to be fought for against the absolute totalitarianism of Germany and the other totalitarian governments. They nevertheless created a world which should never have been allowed to exist in Britain and which only the twentieth century could have called into being. The tribunals before which people such as Middleton Murry's followers appeared were formidable. Their purpose was to find out whether the thoughts of those before them were genuine, and whether they conformed to the rigidly laid down guidelines that enabled the pacifist to remain a pacifist in practice. An idea of the thought processes of those who conducted these inquisitions can be found in the recollections of one tribunal member, Professor Guy Field, published in 1945 and entitled *Pacifism and Conscientious Objectors*. Field served on a tribunal from 1940 until 1944 and wrote his book to justify what he had done; instead he has provided us with a record of the depths to which a free country can sink. Field was a professor of philosophy and, although Orwell himself objected strongly to the pacifists, his creation of the Thought Police showed his opinion of the activities of those in ivory towers who toyed with the fate of ordinary people who were simply more vulnerable or more sincere in their beliefs than their fellow citizens.

The first thing a conscientious objector had to do was write down a statement of his case. As Field remarked this could extend from thirty pages to a single sentence, 'I do not believe in war'. Anyone like Winston Smith who wished to revolt against what was going on around him would find himself sitting at a desk writing down what he thought was wrong with the world that wished to send him to war to kill his fellow man. Countless diaries of the kind Winston wrote must have been started during the war: Field alone heard several thousand cases whilst he sat on the South-Western Tribunal, and all could have been writing desperately to preserve themselves, hiding the incriminating document in case their houses were raided. When the written submissions had been examined for logical precision and then categorised, those writing them were called for interview by the tribunal. These examinations were held in public and the proceedings sometimes appeared in local papers. Professor Field was valued by his colleagues as a skilled interrogator and he used his training as a philosopher to expose the logical errors in the opinions of those who came before him in a voice which, in his book, uncannily resembles O'Brien in his interrogation of Winston in Room 101. Of arguments put forward by people who professed themselves pacifists he remarked:

> It is desirable to point out, without dwelling on it unduly, how very far many pacifist arguments are from reaching the level of Dr Cadoux [a prominent pacifist]. Some, indeed, can only be dismissed as the product of ignorance or confusion of thought.

There can hardly have been a single ordinary person who would *not* be deemed ignorant or confused under public examination by someone of the calibre of Field. He added later:

> We have even had applicants, such is the perversity of which the human mind is capable, who have objected to taking part in this war because Britain had not intervened earlier to check aggression by force.

There were many objections on religious grounds and Field noted with the amused disdain of a philosopher that he had recorded adherents of fifty-one different religious bodies. But

45

there was one ground of objection which is very close to Orwell's thought, and that was 'the supposedly bad effect that war has on our general standards of veracity'. Orwell's original sketch for *Nineteen Eighty-Four* referred to the systematic lying on which society was based in wartime Britain and it remained as a cornerstone of his book. Field found this ground of objection particularly annoying and devoted two pages to tearing it apart. The fact that such bodies as the Anti-Lie Bureau existed and that propaganda reached unheard of heights of duplicity meant nothing to him besides the pleasure of demolishing in logical argument the suggestion that this could be so, or that, if it were, that many more lies were told in peace than in war. As he put it:

> The fact is that any strong emotional attachment to a cause tends to lower one's standards of fairness and accuracy. When we recall some of the propaganda in the period that preceded the present war we might well feel justified in asserting that Truth could not be the first casualty in the war as she had already been fatally injured in the campaign for Peace.

This is the kind of orthodox argument which justified anything, and came particularly well from someone whose job was to determine whether those appealing were telling the *truth* about their beliefs. He went on, clearly aware that he was on delicate ground, to say that what really mattered was whether these lies had any lasting effect after the war was over, suggesting they did not—for those who Field's 'lowered standards of fairness and accuracy' caused to go to war and be killed, or kill others, they could be said to be very lasting indeed. Field even went so far as to argue on similar lines that war brought economic benefit and that the subsequent inflation and unemployment were totally unrelated.

It is necessary to dwell on a person such as Professor Field since he was by no means alone and Orwell's satire of the Thought Police was no doubt aimed at such people as much as at MI5, who of course consulted with tribunals. Today they are concealed within the government apparat, unknown and relatively harmless, and a modern generation could scarcely realise what they were capable of when power was once in their hands. Orwell was fully acquainted with them, and with such as Field because many with whom he kept on personally good terms such as Reg Reynolds were exactly those who suffered these interrogations. Middleton Murry was too old for this kind of attack, but it did not stop his house being raided, and he came very close indeed to detention under the emergency powers regulations. It is possible that his going to his cooperative farm in 1942 and staying in the country was as a result of an order confining him to within five miles of his home. Another noted pacifist who was subjected to such an order was the Duke of Bedford. His pacifism took a particularly virulent form—he was also violently anti-Semitic and a founder of the British People's Party of which Kim Philby's father was a member, suffering detention for it. It was said that the Duke of Bedford could not actually be detained with Sir Oswald Mosley because of the effect it would have on opinion in America; if so that is all that saved him.

This political dimension brings us to the other form of tribunal that operated during the war, that which determined whether detention without trial under regulation 18b was just or not. The tribunal had no powers to order a release and MI5 could over-rule any recommendation which they might make to the Home Secretary, although this was the alleged reason for these tribunals. It was not the actual reason. The tribunals were not held in public, and those appearing before the tribunal had no right to legal representation of any kind. In a particularly Orwellian touch there were actually four members of each tribunal. The fourth member was the MI5 case officer, but since MI5 did not legally exist he was not counted in the total. Three plus one equals three.

The tribunal's purpose appears to have been simply to establish what the defendants thought and to obtain what new information they could. The main reason for thinking this is so is that appeal before the tribunal was compulsory. In fact according to the regulations this was only an option that was open to detainees, but those who did not ask to see the tribunal found that they were called anyway and that an application had been sent in for them. They were brought before the tribunal by force if necessary, and those who took a very strong line were taken to a 'tough' interrogation centre in Ham Common, London. A number of the transcripts of these interrogations have been released, including that of Sir Oswald Mosley himself. At one point he remarked that the tribunal was on a fishing expedition, and this was undoubtedly correct. Parson's pathetic idea of thanking the tribunal for catching him before it was too late would have cut no ice with the 18b tribunals: they found out what they wanted to know and if they failed they knew men who could find out for them.

There are several references in Orwell's writing to 18b. In one of his *Partisan Review* letters at the end of the war after the Labour Party came to power he said:

> In general people of left-wing views are in favour of cont-
> inuing wartime controls; there were even some murmurs
> against the discontinuance of 18b.

Orwell is here putting his finger on one of the great mysteries of the use of 18b, and, indirectly, revealing his own personal fears of what might happen if the Communist Party ever came to power in Britain, or got intimately involved with the Labour Party. The fact was that despite the Nazi-Soviet pact, and the actual cooperation of their propaganda departments, almost no communists were detained under 18b while nearly two thousand of Mosley's men were held in one mass swoop of the senior officials in his party, without any provisions being made for their wives and children unless, like Lady Mosley, the wives were also detained. This was doubly odd as the Communist Party did not keep quiet but gave every support they could to the Nazi war effort, organising strikes in aircraft factories and other vital points in the economy repeatedly. Their newspaper the *Daily Worker* never once praised British troops or made any favourable reference to the war. Worse, they embarked on a campaign in the second half of 1940 which had the sole aim of getting Britain out of the war and setting up a revolutionary government which would negotiate peace immediately. This battle, which Orwell became involved in and which made him enemies lasting for the rest of his life, will now be described in detail.

Orwell's arrival in London coincided with the German advance in Europe, the evacuation at Dunkirk and the threat of invasion. There had been a period of some six weeks during which the fear of invasion dominated all other considerations. When Anthony Eden broadcast a request for men for a force of Local Defence Volunteers, later to be called the Home Guard, Orwell enlisted immediately. After the first fears receded, the Communist Party set in train a campaign which became known as the People's Convention movement. Its manifestos, produced in rapid succession, were all written by D. N. Pritt, the communist Q. C. The final version was called *Forward to a People's Peace*.

The demands of Pritt's programme were uncompromising and entirely in line with the aims of the Nazi-Soviet pact. In the battle of the airwaves German English-language stations, black and white, put over the same message: Peace Now! The fact that this treasonable activity was allowed to continue must have been a calculated act, but no evidence that this was so has ever appeared. It is possible that the senior figures in the cabinet, from Churchill downwards, were unaware of what was going on but someone within the security services certainly knew. And if the decision to do nothing was not one of covert suppression of the information then the matter would be extremely serious, for the case officer involved was Roger Hollis. This is not the place to go over the Hollis case, but the facts are that this movement was allowed to flourish and the *Daily Worker* allowed to continue in publication until the very last moment against the urgent request of the Security Executive that it be suppressed. Orwell would have known nothing of this internal battle at the time, although he may have been informed later. He did however become aware of the People's Convention movement and wrote about it in his diary. His informant is not named and it would be extremely interesting to know who he was:

——is convinced, perhaps rightly, that the danger of the People's Convention racket is much under-estimated and that one must fight back and not ignore it. He says that thousands of simple minded people are taken in by the appealing programme of the People's Convention and do not realise that it is a defeatist manoeuvre intended to help Hitler. He quoted a letter from the Dean of Canterbury who said 'I want you to understand that I am wholeheartedly for winning the war, and that I believe Winston Churchill to be the only possible leader for us until the war is over' and nevertheless supported the People's Convention.

Orwell became involved in this fight by going around tearing down posters advertising the Convention which had suddenly appeared all over London, printed at great cost. In writing about his actions he said that this was the first time he had done such a thing, going on to reminisce about his time in Barcelona when he had gone around chalking up *'Visca POUM'* after the organisation he fought with had been suppressed. Clearly Orwell thought he was involved in just such a fight. Revolution *was* close and it would not be the revolution he hoped for in *The Lion and the Unicorn* but a Stalinist version. Whoever it was that warned Orwell, and whatever the reality or otherwise of the threat, the image of Orwell going around wartime London tearing down posters is a strong one.

There is further evidence that Orwell was not alone in his actions but if he was working with some official backing, whose it was is not entirely clear. His diary is understandably skimped at this period, for it does not mention any of his articles where some of this evidence appears, or his actions in connection with the Home Guard. These have been widely misinterpreted; it has even been suggested that he saw it as a revolutionary force! The position was almost exactly the reverse of this, as his statements in the various articles he wrote at the time make quite clear. He wrote, for example:

> The communists, the ILP, and all their kind can parrot 'Arms for the Workers', but they cannot put a rifle into the workers' hands. The Home Guard can and does. The moral for any socialist who is reasonably fit and can spare a certain amount of time is obvious . . . Any socialist who obtains influence in the Home Guard will do it by being conspicuously obedient, efficient and self-sacrificing.

Any lingering doubt about the message that Orwell was giving is dispelled by another article he wrote a few days before the Convention actually gathered for the London *Evening Standard*. Under the headline DON'T LET COLONEL BLIMP RUIN THE HOME GUARD, (completely misleading since his message was to get anyone on the left who harboured revolutionary feelings into the Home Guard under military discipline), he wrote:

> Even as it stands the Home Guard could only exist in a country where men feel themselves free. The totalitarian states can do great things, but there is one thing they cannot do, they cannot give the factory worker a rifle and tell him to take it home and keep it in his bedroom. THAT RIFLE HANGING ON THE WALL OF THE WORKING-CLASS FLAT OR LABOURER'S COTTAGE IS THE SYMBOL OF DEMOCRACY. IT IS OUR JOB TO SEE IT STAYS THERE.

These urgent messages, at the very time the *Daily Worker* was carrying articles by Claud Cockburn (under the pseudonym Frank Pitcairn) urging soldiers to go back to their barracks and start insurrection immediately, arming the workers, can have had only one purpose—to neutralise any possible danger

51

of revolution by getting all those workers who wanted to arm themselves into the Home Guard where their patriotism and respect for democracy would bring them back to their senses. For such appeals to appear in the *Evening Standard* Orwell must have had official backing—it would have been quite impossible to publish such material unless he had. Again it is not possible to know how this was done, or who he was working with. But it is certain that those in the Communist Party who were behind the People's Convention would have known who their enemy was. When the Convention was actually held it was a failure. And if those organising it wanted someone to blame then the campaign in which Orwell took so prominent part would be an obvious target.

Orwell's reputation suffered from this involvement even after his death, for one of the main critics of Orwell was the academic and political activist Raymond Williams. At the time of the People's Convention he was a Cambridge undergraduate and the leader of the supporters of the Nazi-Soviet pact. He was the organiser of the People's Convention movement in Cambridge and when their meetings were banned he led the delegation in protest. His involvement in what was objectively pro-Nazi propaganda at such a crucial time must have coloured the rest of his life. When he attacked Orwell later, and increasingly as he grew older, the fact that they were on opposite sides at this crucial time must have counted for a lot. If he had supported the revolution then assuredly Orwell had betrayed it, worse, proclaiming himself a socialist all the while.

Orwell's main forum for his views at this time was the magazine *Tribune*. Others who contributed to it in the campaign against the People's Convention included John Strachey, an ex-communist, later to become a minister in the post-war Labour government. The significance of the whole affair for *Nineteen Eighty-Four* is clear. If, at the height of a war, the Communist Party could dupe people into supporting a campaign against their own country that played directly into the hands of the Nazi and Stalinist totalitarian systems, then the dangers of some such operation being mounted against the Labour government, even with people such as Strachey in it, who had lived through the Convention and knew what the British communists were capable of, were very great. It may be that Orwell sensed through his experience at the BBC and elsewhere that there really were people such as 'Stalin's Englishmen', Burgess, Maclean and Philby, and a host of others who never made the headlines. That his actions in 1941 also brought back to him his experience in Spain, when communist betrayal nearly cost him his life, would only have heightened his awareness of the dangers.

Orwell's suspicions about the weakness of the authorities in their fight against communists in Britain must have been raised by the fact that, despite all that happened, and the closing down of the *Daily Worker*, there were still no detentions under 18b. Claud Cockburn's articles were such that he should have been detained immediately, as could most of those working on the paper with him. That they were not may have been a deliberate act by the authorities who knew that Russia might come in on Britain's side and they should do nothing to upset Stalin, but there was always the feeling that some other force was protecting them.

The People's Convention movement carried on after the failure of the Convention itself. Amongst those who appeared on the platform had been J. B. S. Haldane and, astonishingly, Indira Gandhi, later to become Prime Minister of India and to be assassinated by her own body guards. Her presence at the Convention has never been explained—nor how she came across Europe from Switzerland to Britain to attend it. Only the actual invasion of Russia by Germany brought it to an end, and then in hilarious circumstances which Orwell described in his diary entry for 6 July, 1941:

> The People's Convention have voted full support for the government and demand 'vigorous prosecution of the war'—this only a fortnight after they were demanding a 'people's peace'.

The story is going around that, when the news of Hitler's invasion of Russia reached a New York cafe where some communists were talking, one of them who had gone out to the lavatory returned to find that the 'party line' had changed in his absence.

And here clearly is the origin of Orwell's portrait of the party speaker in *Nineteen Eighty-Four* who is capable of changing his line in tune with that of the party without even breaking the syntax of a sentence he was half way through speaking.

The harsh political battles described briefly in this chapter were indeed the reality that underlay the basically corrupt literary world described earlier. Orwell's disparaging references to the Cafe Royal set have to be taken in this context; he took life more seriously.

Besides the literary cliques and the political struggle there was one new element that entered Orwell's life at this point and that was the radio. In an autobiographical sketch he sent to an American magazine at this time he said he disliked the radio and it seems that he did not own one when he lived in London—in any event he and Eileen would frequently go to their neighbourhood pub to hear the news on the set there—but he was considered eccentric in this view. One person who shared a review spot with him on the *New Statesman*, Desmond Hawkins, besides being a writer himself, was doing a series of programmes for the BBC. He asked Orwell to appear in one of them and surprisingly Orwell agreed. His life took another turn.

CHAPTER SIX

Orwell at the BBC

The constant background to every party member's life in *Nineteen Eighty-Four*, indeed the only thing that gave their lives purpose, was the continuous stream of news-flashes and broadcasts giving details of the progress of the war. If Orwell featured in the book it was not in the persona of Winston Smith, Ministry of Truth worker, but as the writer of those news briefings, for this was how he spent a good part of each week during the two years he spent with the BBC. Some of the detail is borrowed from German broadcasts that he saw every day in the monitors' reports: it was the Germans who heralded every announcement of victory—and they were always victories—with grand fanfares. But for the rest even the incidents of fighting in *Nineteen Eighty-Four* in south India on the Malabar front refer directly to his work broadcasting to millions of Indians in just such places.

We have seen Orwell wanted to take part in the war effort and had been bitterly disappointed when he could not get into uniform. But it is astonishing to find him in the front line in the most modern kind of political warfare, radio propaganda. Before this war he had tended to look back to a golden age before the First World War—his book *Coming Up for Air* is a classic statement of the evils of the twentieth century. The coming of war had revived his old loyalties, but then plunged him even further into a world he despised. He did not even like radio, and yet here he was rubbing his face into the very worst of the world of lies and deceit in which the totalitarians were passed masters. This problem is ignored by his biographers, although Bernard Crick remarks that there may have been some guile used in recruiting him. He dismisses Orwell's work at the BBC simply as wasted years. How had he been chosen? And did his accepting this kind of work merely reflect his impossible financial position which was tearing his personal life apart? Or again was it a reward of some kind for his actions in the fight against the People's Convention movement when his actual political position, so different from most who had fought in Spain, had become plain.

The element of guile that Professor Crick found in Orwell's appointment referred to the fact that Orwell's books were actually banned in India and it was known he stood for independence for the sub-continent absolutely. Anyone now reading the sections on India in *The Lion and the Unicorn* would find Orwell's view curiously old-fashioned, especially in the light of what actually happened when Labour gave India its freedom. The speed of the transfer was faster than anything Orwell was looking for even in his most revolutionary phase:

> In the age of the tank and the bombing plane, backward agricultural countries like India and the African colonies can no more be independent than can a cat or a dog. Had any Labour Government come into office with a clear majority and then proceeded to grant India anything that could be truly called independence, India would simply have been absorbed by Japan or divided between Japan and Russia.

Orwell saw a proper aim for any Labour government to be the creation of a 'positive' imperial policy aimed at transforming the Empire into a federation of socialist states. He felt that the British, particularly engineers and so on, should remain in the country for at least a decade.

The key element in his thinking here is that he saw the threat of a Japanese take-over in India as the major danger. There were two million Indian troops fighting under the British flag and any attempt at independence would create total chaos amongst them and leave the back door open for the Japanese and Russians. In historical terms the shrewdness of this view can be seen in the role Russia actually did play in post-independence India. The authorities at the time would have seen Orwell as an ideal recruit to broadcast to India if he wished to do so. The banning of his book *Burmese Days* in India probably had as much to do with not wanting to sap the morale of *white* residents of India as with anything the native population would get from the book. And the instincts to censor books were as well-developed then as at any time in Britain's history.

Orwell agreed to take on the task. He had first broadcast with Desmond Hawkins in a series called 'The Writer in the Witness Box' and had gone on to do a series of four talks for broadcast to India. These talks can be seen now as establishing in his own mind his moral position and one can see that he was saying that he would broadcast, but about literary subjects and on his own terms. There were two literary talks on Gerard Manley Hopkins and Tolstoy and two overtly political talks, 'The Frontiers of Art and Propaganda' and 'Literature and Totalitarianism'. In these talks he goes over clearly and concisely what his own views of the change in literary criticism had been in the thirties. Those who had revolted against the aesthetic view in favour of the political and had followed the broad Marxist line found that when the Nazi-Soviet pact was announced they were in a blind alley. As Orwell put it '. . . you cannot really sacrifice your intellectual integrity for the sake of a political creed—or at least you cannot do so and remain a writer.' In joining the BBC, Orwell was obviously very clear in his own mind that he was not sacrificing his political integrity as we can see now he was not.

There is a further element in these talks which is of interest in terms of the development of *Nineteen Eighty-Four*. In refusing to sacrifice his intellectual integrity the writer inevitably finds himself isolated. Not quite perhaps *The Last Man* but one who feels his individuality more than those with the comfortable blanket of an orthodoxy wrapped around them. Remarking that 'we live in an age in which the autonomous individual is ceasing to exist . . .' he went on to point out that the existence of the individual was taken for granted, and that this idea was linked with intellectual honesty. He cites Shakespeare, as he does in *Nineteen Eighty-Four*, with his maxim 'To thine own self be true'. He did not think that the failure of literature and the loss of individual freedom was inevitable. Although totalitarian states had gone beyond telling people what not to think, censoring works, by telling them emphatically what they *had* to think, he did not think its worldwide spread was unavoidable:

> I believe that the hope of literature's survival lies in those countries in which liberalism has struck its deepest roots, to the non-military countries, western Europe and the Americas, India and China . . . Whoever feels the value of literature, whoever sees the central part it plays in the development of human history, must also see the life and death necessity of resisting totalitarianism, whether it is imposed on us from without or from within.

Despite these clear statements of his integrity there was one flaw in his decision to commit himself to the government's propaganda team and he would have realised this as soon as he saw the first script he had to broadcast, for on the top of each sheet were the two censors' stamps, one for security and one for policy, without which the broadcast could not go ahead. In his essay he had said, clearly:

> The first thing we ask of a writer is that he shall not tell lies, that he shall say what he really thinks and what he really feels.

Censorship falls into a grey area on this delicate question. As we shall see in the next chapter, Orwell resigned from the BBC with a letter which specifically referred to not being made to say anything in which he did not believe, but that it is not quite the same thing as being allowed to say everything he believed in. The tension between those two positions in the end forced Orwell out of the BBC and provided one of the central motivating forces behind the writing of *Nineteen Eighty-Four*.

The four talks were done for broadcasting to India because Desmond Hawkins had been acting as a consultant for the India Service programmes. He found at this time that he could not carry on with what was really a full-time job and it was decided that Orwell should carry on the job as a fully fledged BBC employee. If there was any 'guile' shown in his recruitment then it must have been operating at an early stage in his connection with the BBC since he had worked with Hawkins from the first. Indeed it would have depended on the chance circumstance of Hawkins doing review work with Orwell at the *New Statesman*. It is at least as likely that Orwell knew Hawkins' position and saw the opportunity to find a niche for himself. Speculation is probably fruitless. What is worth doing is examining the programmes Orwell actually did, concentrating on the literary work which was a *sine qua non* for his agreeing to broadcast to India at all.

In his talk on 'Literature and Totalitarianism' Orwell mentioned India and China. It seems from this that the intention to appoint him had already at least been discussed, since at the same time someone was found to do the China talks—William Empson—and he attended the same training school session as Orwell. Empson remained a working colleague of Orwell's right through his time at the BBC and stayed on considerably longer, not having the same moral imperatives that made him kick against the censorship and political cant current at the time. Their colleague in the home talks department was someone with even more deft political footwork, none other than Guy Burgess. Burgess worked in a different building from Orwell but their paths crossed frequently, most often over interviews with MPs and the reporting of debates. Orwell had an Indian political correspondent, Princess Indira of Kapurthala, and interviews would be done with people chosen jointly by Burgess and Orwell. On another level Orwell proved very successful in getting literary figures to broadcast for him, so much so that professional jealousy soon intervened. Burgess had a very high reputation as a producer and it annoyed him to discover that, for example, E. M. Forster was happy to broadcast for Orwell but declined to do talks for him. He put a typically petulant memorandum on record. This was a world that Orwell knew nothing of—no doubt his ability to attract speakers stemmed from his being obviously candid and straightforward. He was to work with Burgess on several occasions over the next few years.

Empson was a different case. The author of the famous book *Seven Types of Ambiguity*, he was a well-known intellectual and authority on China. Among his enthusiasms was Basic English and Sime (in *Nineteen Eighty-Four*) has been seen as a good caricature of him, talking about newspeak as Empson talked about Basic, one of his pet subjects, in the basement canteen of the overseas section of the BBC. Orwell worked with him happily enough but Empson did not agree with Orwell on a wide variety of points and later carried his dislike through to overtly patronising criticism of Orwell's *Animal Farm* and *Nineteen Eighty-Four*, perhaps recognising how close Orwell's satire came to the truth. He and Orwell worked in the same room, each in a cubicle which corresponds closely to those in which Winston Smith works in *Nineteen Eighty-Four*.

The extent of Orwell's work at the BBC can be seen in the material discovered in 1984 in the BBC's archives where it had lain unrecognised for nearly forty years. A wide variety of his talks, letters and news broadcasts were subsequently published and the reader can judge how much Orwell's normal style was affected by working for the new medium. As has been remarked already, the weekly news broadcasts feature in *Nineteen Eighty-Four* with only slight variations.

Apart from these most obvious references to 'victories' and 'fighting on the Malabar front' there is the less obvious reference to the state of mind Orwell must soon have reached when writing these pieces. He describes Winston seeing in his mind a map of the fighting with arrows sweeping across India showing Eurasian forces being cut off, or victorious. Just such images must have filled Orwell's mind as he struggled to produce the masterly synopsis of World War news which was broadcast each week. There could hardly be a greater contrast between the literary world and this kind of reporting. Today, certainly, no one person would be called on to do both kinds of work and it is doubtful if anyone could be found able to do it.

From the first Orwell ran a series of scientific programmes. The origin of this interest is not clear, however we have seen how he had earlier tried to enroll in the government training programme for machine draftsmen, and his sister, Avril, and Inez Holden both worked in factories in London through the blitz. One of these series was called 'A.D. 2000'. Its purpose was to look at what life in India would be like then from a variety of viewpoints but all scientifically based. It was a first look into the future for Orwell instead of his more normal nostalgic view of the past. It is interesting also in its use of a simple date for the title, rather than a phrase or quotation, though he did finally use *Nineteen Eighty-Four* rather than A.D. 1984.

Orwell's experience of scientists was not always happy. As we shall see he attempted to use J. B. S. Haldane, despite his affiliation with the People's Convention movement which Orwell so much hated. He also tried to use J. D. Bernal, the Marxist scientist, apparently without realising his political position. Behind the scenes Burgess exerted pressure on Bernal which resulted in his suddenly telling Orwell he could no longer be anchorman for his series. This was a major incident with later repercussions explored in chapter twelve. He was also seeing H. G. Wells a lot at this time. Although there was a well-known argument here also, a broad scientific view of the world would have harked back to the earlier Wells whom Orwell greatly admired. It is hard for us to realise it now, but Russia was at the time thought to be far ahead of Britain in scientific achievement, a belief that people such as Haldane and Bernal fervently supported and promulgated. Orwell seems to have gone along with them to some degree, but he always saw beyond the scientific achievements to the political reality—the totalitarian mind of Stalin and his cohorts.

More interesting still, from the point of view of *Nineteen Eighty-Four*, are the literary talks he wrote and the other authors he got to work with him on them. A separate volume of these talks and his correspondence at the BBC was published which enable a careful study to be made of the work which immediately preceded the writing of *Animal Farm* and which provided much of the substance of *Nineteen Eighty-Four* itself, apart from the influence of his scientific talk series which looked even further ahead to the year 2000.

It is not surprising that two of Orwell's literary talks should be about Jack London and Swift, both of whom he would write about again. His talk on London draws attention once more to London's book *The Iron Heel* and its prophecy of fascism, but adds the detail that the book was better known outside the English-speaking countries and had a particular vogue on the continent ten or fifteen years before Hitler had come to power. With his own book he was going to be looking forward only thirty or forty years rather than the centuries in *The Iron Heel* but on the other hand he obviously hoped *Nineteen Eighty-Four* would have an influence of the kind he thought London's book had had at some time between the book's appearance and the year 1984 itself. At the same time his talk on Swift, which took the form of an imaginary conversation with him—the idea was not Orwell's incidentally, he was doing one in a series of such talks for another producer—showed that he was fully conscious of Swift's model. His statement on the place *Gulliver's Travels* had had in his life is important for its complete commitment:

I believe *Gulliver's Travels* has meant more to me than any other book ever written. I can't remember when I first read it, I must have been eight years old at the most, and it has lived with me ever since so that I suppose a year has never passed without my re-reading at least part of it.

And clearly he was reading it at the time, for his dialogue shows a complete and very recent understanding of the text. With the fusing together of these literary sources and the work on a series set in the future (albeit 2000 rather than 1984) one can almost see the transformation of the idea he had for the 'family saga' in three parts into the kind of book he finally wrote.

After straightforward talks and essays Orwell became more adventurous. He tried a literary experiment—and used that scientific term to describe it to E. M. Forster—the writing of a story in five parts each by different authors. He presumably wanted to test his idea that authors were losing their individuality and that even fiction could be written to order. He thought the experiment a failure, which paradoxically meant that it had proved him wrong; however much you tried people retained their own individual traits. The story is interesting to us for the various incidents which make it a direct source for *Nineteen Eighty-Four* and which point also to other roots in the real world around him at the time.

E. M. Forster might seem the least likely person to become involved in a literary experiment of this kind, but he wrote to Orwell saying how much he enjoyed it: 'It represented my first attempt at fiction for many years, and I enjoyed doing it'. He had earlier referred to the task as being 'scarcely my cup of beer' but most interesting of all were his comments on the script and the final comments which came at the end of the last episode of the story which seems to have been written by him but with strong input from Orwell. He said in his letter agreeing to do the story that the theme had been messed about 'by the Spanish expedition' as he put it, referring to Inez Holden's contribution:

> I am afraid that any denouement will seem unreal and can only be handled 'cleverly'. I have an idea and will do my best with it.

And at the end of the story he made this final comment:

> I expect there are better endings to the story, and in particular that something more ought to have been done with that woman in overalls [who appeared in the first episode by Orwell]. But I could not work her in, and since the scenery prescribed was falling houses and the blitz I turned to the character that best typifies destruction . . .

Story by Five Authors was also Orwell's first attempt at fiction in wartime and the reference to the woman in overalls here might equally well have come from Orwell, and perhaps did, since they talked about the story at length. The moment in the story when the girl in overalls suddenly kisses Moss with a kiss that tastes of plaster occurs also in *Nineteen Eighty-Four* when Julia kisses Winston. This is no doubt one of those fragments of reality which Orwell wove into all his fiction but if Winston/Moss was Orwell in real life who was Julia? The obvious suggestion here is Inez Holden. She features as one of the authors of the story but the exact connection, like that between Empson and Sime will be looked at later on here. What is clear is that however small this scrap of fiction was, written in the blackest days of the war, it provided a seed for future work and this seed struck down roots into the rest of his wartime experience.

Towards the end of his time with the BBC Orwell embarked on a new kind of work, the adaptation of stories and books for wireless, in those days called featurisation. He wrote them very quickly, weighed under by administrative work that had been given him after he was stopped from doing news summaries. In a letter at the time he said he wrote them in a day. He was conscious that they were a brilliant achievement that he was proud of, for after the war he wrote to Rayner Heppenstall expressing regret that they had not been re-broadcast. He had had an illicit recording made of them which unfortunately he had lost and wanted to hear it again and make a fresh recording. For us the most interesting of these adaptations was one of Ignazio Silone's *The Fox*, a political fable set in a farm in Switzerland on the Italian border. One of the pigs is named after Mussolini, although the fox in the story is the central character, forever attempting to steal honest people's chickens. And there is also an Italian staying with the farmer's family who is in reality also a fox, spying for the fascists whilst pretending to be a friend.

This adaptation was only published for the first time in 1985 but it was finished and broadcast a few weeks before Orwell left the BBC and started work on *Animal Farm*. The influence of this adaptation on *Animal Farm* is obvious at two levels. First there is the setting and the use of an animal in a political allegory. Second, there is the less obvious factor of the great gulf which separates *Animal Farm* stylistically from any work he had done previously. The speed with which the book was written and its conciseness surely come directly from skills developed in his work doing the featurisations of *The Fox* and the other stories. This was literary work, and the fact that he insisted that he do such work when broadcasting to India, not simply political propaganda, is a measure of his integrity and strength of will. He reaped the benefit by having to hand at the end a mind which had not been deadened as had those of so many others who became embroiled in the wartime bureaucratic nightmare of the BBC and the MOI.

Some time after leaving the BBC Orwell referred to the shelves full of rubbish he wrote whilst he was there, and when he left he spoke of feeling like an orange that had been trodden on by a very dirty boot. All this was true, and his resentment and fear for England generally if all were subjected to that regime fired him to write his great satire. But the BBC he spoke of then was not the relatively sane literary world we have looked at in this chapter but something quite different.

CHAPTER SEVEN

The Censorship Culture

E. M. Forster is best known today for his classic *A Passage to India*; it was already a classic in Orwell's time and was the main reason for his being asked to broadcast for the Indian service. But there was then another side to his character. He was a frequently outspoken critic of censorship in Britain and his feelings led him to commit himself openly by writing pieces such as the preface to the controversial *The Banned Books of England* by Alec Craig. It was this kind of censorship that led to Orwell's house being raided, although neither he nor Forster seem to have been aware of the wider implications of the mail censorship that lay behind such raids which have been mentioned earlier. Orwell no doubt talked to Forster on such matters and this would explain an unusual lapse for him, namely specific reference to the censorship of a script Forster had written, the final episode of the *Story by Five Authors*. Urging him to get his script in by a certain time Orwell added:

> We should like to have your script some time on Thursday if possible . . . I'm sorry about this but it has to be censored first thing Friday morning.

It is worth emphasising that this was censorship of *fiction* not news, politics, or current affairs. Technically even this statement by Orwell acted as a breach of the Official Secrets Act although it was well known amongst contributors that their work would be censored.

The method by which this censorship was carried out was relatively simple and is essentially the same as that used today when editing radio and television programmes. It had been developed from the earliest days of broadcasting when considerations of timing, and the tendency for people to be struck dumb when confronted by a microphone, even though they knew exactly what they wanted to say, led to full scripting of talks and news and other programmes. Announcers became professional actors who could deliver lines with spontaneity, conviction and style. Today the invention of the autocue, invisible to the audience, makes it seem to the average viewer as if the announcer, or speaker, is talking directly to them. In fact the script is there, usually written by someone else. It is a simple step to censor a script, whether it is in front of a radio announcer or on the autocue before a television presenter.

There was some complication when it came to talks involving more than one person, but here again the need to write scripts to an exact timing had led to the development of suitable scripting techniques. There were producers who could take a fifteen-minute essay by an author and a further fifteen minutes from an interviewer and weave them together into a convincing dialogue lasting half an hour without any difficulty at all. Even the two participants would usually agree a splendid job had been done. And the end result could be censored whenever convenient. The equivalent of this on television, practised today, is to have an interview which is then intercut with 'questions' from the person conducting the programme. The traditions of censorship linger on within the system, for the temptation to cut out crucial statements, or use a sequence of fragments of an interview to make the person being interviewed say something he may well not agree with is, to many, irresistible.

In an actual case one producer remarked that to deprive him of this right would be an interference with his editorial freedom. In fact what he was doing was exactly what happened during the war, using identical methods. A speaker, usually an author such as Forster, wrote his text and the censor adapted it to make him say what it was thought desirable he should say. The most he could do was to refuse to read his own text, and that often did happen, although the reasons given varied. As we shall see others such as J. B. S. Haldane made a practice of simply departing from the set text as they were broadcasting live. The authorities were aware of this danger and had what was called then a switch censor who sat by the microphone with a copy of the script and turned it off if the script was departed from in any way.

The skills which Orwell developed in judging how long a script would take and in editing other people's scripts so that they could go forward for censorship were no doubt skills he would rather not possess, but as long as he was not obliged to say anything untruthful he learned to live with it. Those who have criticised him for this and who remarked on the incongruity of Orwell's instructions 'For Censorship Please', which appeared on his scripts (one is illustrated here) and coming from one who stood for freedom of speech before anything, have not looked at the many legitimate reasons which he might have had. His foremost purpose was not to help the totalitarian enemy in any way whatsoever. A simple example will illustrate the most basic problems.

Early in the bombing campaigns there was considerable difficulty in deciding what news could be released about such incidents as the bombing of hospitals. At first it was thought desirable that the enemy should not know what they had hit, and a statement would be broadcast saying that a hospital in the London area had suffered damage. However, this resulted in the switchboards of every hospital being jammed with calls from anxious relatives. Not to mention the news at all would have aroused misgivings amongst the public to whom the fact of the BBC being uncensored was an article of faith—it was what we were fighting for. A compromise was arranged with a special number being given for people to phone, much as is done today.

There were nevertheless wider reasons why radio had to be censored on a massive scale, and these involved not just the broadcasts themselves but the newspapers. Once Europe had been over-run by Germany there was no possibility of news being obtained other than through radio broadcasts. The BBC monitored these from all over the world and published details in a daily *Summary of World Broadcasts* (SWB). This appeared in a strictly limited print run and was described as secret; however it was in itself censored although this was kept most strictly secret and few knew of it. The newspapers were amongst those on the Summary's limited distribution list and used it as a prime source that substituted for the correspondents they now lacked. This censorship, combined with censorship of all incoming cables, meant that the press had no source of news that was not censored. Further, as far as domestic matters were concerned, they were restricted by the 'D' notice system which still operates in Britain to the present day, preventing mention of a wide range of matters.

Orwell worked for an overseas broadcasting station and all the restrictions and censorship systems were applied to ensure first that nothing got out that could help the enemy, and secondly that those who listened in Britain, as some could, would not hear anything that they could not get on the home services. Orwell frequently read the *Summary of World Broadcasts* and mentioned this in letters, saying in one, for example, that he often read transcripts of Ezra Pound's broadcasts there. Careful reading of his news broadcasts shows that he frequently used this material and actually answered it. The main reason for restricting the circulation of the *Summary of World Broadcasts* was that it contained full transcripts of the 'black' propaganda stations. These broadcast in English and pretended to be based in England and were the main source of the Haw-Haw rumours that were mentioned in chapter two. Between them Orwell and Eileen would have had an ideal opportunity to piece together a complete picture of the world at war, and the place of censorship and the MOI censorship systems. It is unlikely that Orwell was able to bring home the SWB but he would have talked about it and Eileen would have known of its existence.

There was one other area where Eileen's world overlapped Orwell's and that was internal mail censorship of the kind mentioned earlier, with an example from the Ministry of Food. Orwell came across it because the BBC was one of those organisations deemed to have a need to know, as was noticed in the incident mentioned in chapter four. They got mail circulated to them, actually in transit, which had information relating to broadcasts they were putting out. The name of one of Orwell's superiors is on a distribution list in the relevant file, and Orwell would have been told of the information obtained from these 'intercepts' even if he did not know its source. But one of his BBC colleagues at the time, and at the same level, knew letters were being circulated in this way and described in detail to the author exactly what happened and it would be unlikely for Orwell not to know also. His department was a very small one.

A full picture thus emerges of Orwell's involvement in the actual censorship of texts. All that he wrote was censored twice, once for policy and once for security; all that was written for him or that he edited was censored in the same way, and finally he had the benefit of the censorship system in being able to see restricted summaries of enemy and neutral broadcasts which formed the basis of much that was only hinted at in the press, together with knowledge of, if not access to, the most secret of the information sources, intercepted mail with comments on his broadcasts, for example, which he had a 'need to know'. Beyond this there was, for a broadcaster, one further question: who could he ask to broadcast in the first place?

Although in theory producers were free to ask who they wanted to do their programmes, in practice there were several restrictions. There was a special procedure for asking famous speakers which had to be followed. It consisted simply of checking with one of the BBC's controllers. The original purpose had been to shield well-known public figures from continual enquiries. However, some public figures were also people with political purposes whose very appearance on radio might have some wider significance. Then there were others who had been a cause of trouble in the past. Many of the procedures were those which any prudent private business might adopt, but the political factors were not in this category. On one occasion, for example, Orwell wanted to use Sir Richard Acland whom he knew. He was told that he could, but not if he was going to speak on his party, the Common Wealth Party. Beyond these considerations there was what was known colloquially as 'the black list'. This was supposed not to exist but Orwell had bitter personal experience of it.

Although Orwell despised the People's Convention and all it stood for he was not one to deny someone the right to their say simply because he disagreed with them. A good example of Orwell's struggles with the powers that be was over J. B. S. Haldane whom he asked to do a talk. His first step was to approach his superior Rushbrook-Williams saying he wanted to use Haldane. Rushbrook-Williams wrote to his superior R. A. Rendall (Assistant Controller Overseas) asking if he could be used, making the revealing remark 'Is he banned? I can't find out if he is a member of the Communist Party or not—no one quite seems to know'. Rendall in turn sent it to J. B. Clarke (Controller Overseas) who replied in a minute which revealed how close to the wind Orwell had pushed his colleagues (and superiors):

i.   There is no general ban on anyone, each case being judged on its merits.
ii. There's no blacklist.
iii. In this case are we really sure that JBSH is the *best* man for this subject? I have personal doubts.
iv. Having regard to past difficulties, are we satisfied that this is a case in which we want to deal with temperamental difficulties over script?

Rendall sent this back down the line with the comment that

they had had previous difficulties with Haldane, 'seldom for any good reason', but saying he could probably get permission if the point was pressed. Orwell did press and Haldane duly did his broadcast. Orwell had done Haldane a great service in getting him back to the microphone and had also learnt exactly how far the censorship and banning of speakers went. It is revealing that the Overseas Controller felt it necessary to say there was no blacklist when he had not been asked. Rushbrook-Williams' 'Is he banned?' tells us exactly how the system worked. Orwell did himself no good by pressing such cases, particularly as Haldane was well known as a man who would produce his own script just as he sat at the microphone and read from that, or ad lib, or argue fiercely over the slightest alteration. There is a further possibility in the interpretation of Orwell's act and that is that he wished to see if Communist Party members *could* get through, knowing that if the authorities checked on who was asking, he above all would be free of any suspicion of having communist leanings. The angle of his enquiry can be seen over another speaker he asked for: Aneurin Bevan. Bevan was a director of *Tribune* and one of Orwell's keen supporters there both at the time of the People's Convention and later. Politically he was a controversial figure but without the slightest suggestion that he was a communist. It is therefore particularly interesting that whereas Orwell succeeded with Haldane he failed with Bevan. Although the subject is still shrouded in mystery it is clear that Bevan was one of those who, in the words of the controller 'would be better left alone'—without any mention of a blacklist of course.

What Orwell may well have been trying to establish was whether there was a political blacklist and how it was that communist speakers could get to the microphone when others such as Bevan had difficulty. Suggestions that the BBC was under some covert communist influence were common then, as they have been subsequently. Those who ridiculed the idea got a tremendous shock when Burgess, talks editor and the man who ran 'The Week in Westminster' and had had as much unofficial 'power' as anyone in the BBC, defected to Moscow. Orwell had a good reason for making this point when he did, in October 1943, for he had himself come under direct fire for evading the censorship regulations and on a specific issue: that of criticising Stalin and Soviet policy.

Besides his usual news broadcasts for the Indian service Orwell would occasionally broadcast to the Far East, covering Malaya, Burma and beyond. On 4 June 1943 Orwell succumbed to the temptation offered by a new and inexperienced censor to let fly a broadside on Stalin's abolition of the comintern. The text has not survived, but it is clear from comment in the papers circulated afterwards that he took an extremely jaundiced view of this attempt of Stalin's to gain favour with his allies. Complaint was made immediately chiefly from the Russian desk at the MOI. J.B. Clarke, the Controller Overseas was obliged to make an abject apology to the Director General of the BBC. He specifically referred to the reason for Orwell's choice for such work:

Orwell was allowed to step into the breach because there was strong external evidence that he was well known and trusted in Burma where it was hoped we would influence an important section of the potential audience.

His memorandum had begun by apologising for 'several serious errors of judgement betrayed by this talk'.

Whether Orwell had been chosen from the very beginning because of the influence he would have it is clear that when asked to broadcast to Burma he was being used, and he knew he was. His response was typical and he can have been in no doubt in the aftermath that he had made a lasting enemy in J. B. Clarke. He must have realised that his position was becoming untenable and, indeed, he could not continue in good conscience. But walking away from such a job, especially in wartime, was not easy; the average person would have thought it both impossible to do, because of the highly secret information he held, and also plain mad unless he had some very secure berth to go to. Orwell seems to have taken the path of pressing the censorship question to its logical conclusion. His next head-on collision was again over the question of whether a speaker was banned or not; the speaker was Kingsley Martin, editor of the *New Statesman* through which Orwell had obtained his introduction to the BBC in the first place.

Kingsley Martin was banned from broadcasting after an incident in 1941 involving a programme intended to be broadcast to America and Canada in the 'Answering You' series. There had been a question submitted by the editor of the Toronto *Saturday Night* on 18b. Martin had been approached by the BBC as a well known critic of left views who would normally, it was said, oppose the imposition of 18b but was in fact prepared to come down in favour of it. It says much for the 'doublethink' of the BBC at this time that such a request, conditional on his giving an agreed answer, could be seen as freedom of speech. The request was doubly disingenuous because it was the right wing who had been detained under 18b when the left wing were allowed to run free; naturally Kingsley Martin would be happy to support it. However there had been a previous talk on 18b which the Home Office had objected to and it was decided to postpone Martin's talk for a week whilst the position was made clear. Martin knew nothing of this but became suspicious and then cried off. He was thenceforth regarded as unusable, until Orwell started using him regularly in the summer of 1943, without consulting anyone above him in the hierarchy. At this point J. B. Clarke discovered that he was being used and demanded to know what was behind it. He could not have chosen a worse moment to raise the query, for almost immediately Kingsley Martin obliged by doing a talk, entirely outside his talk's supposed area, of direct political sensitivity.

The subject of the talk was education, then a matter of much discussion prior to the publication in 1944 of Butler's education act. Clarke had insisted that the Assistant Controller for the Home Service, Burgess's superior, be consulted about the content of the talk. This was highly unusual and Orwell found himself having a fierce row with this eminent personage. In the words of Clarke's memorandum on what happened: 'Blair [he had previously called him Orwell] on consulting A.C.(H) seemed to show scant respect for the normal courtesy and discipline appropriate to an organisation such as ours over some points that were raised by A.C.(H).' There was further heated discussion over what had occurred and Orwell did not come well out of the battle. What must have been galling was that, as in the case of Haldane, he had stuck his neck out for someone with whose opinion he did not at all agree only to find them cause him the greatest problems. The matter ended, within the Indian service, by a brief memo from Rushbrook-Williams:

> We cannot risk any more trouble over Kingsley Martin, and I'd be grateful if you could get Blair's cooperation to ensure that the suggested precautions are in fact observed.

This incident proved to be the last straw. In a letter to his friend Rayner Heppenstall on 24 August Orwell said that he was definitely leaving the BBC. Even if he had had any last minute reservations Kingsley Martin hammered the final nail in his coffin by broadcasting a talk for Orwell on 30 August on 'The Freedom of the Press in Wartime'. Orwell left immediately on two weeks' annual leave and returned with his mind made up. He resigned on 24 September. The letter he wrote has been frequently published however it is reprinted here as a precise indication of Orwell's state of mind, and the sharp contrast with his actual reasons for going which, as this chapter has shown, were in reality completely tied up with the question of censorship of opinion, a central question also in the satire in *Nineteen Eighty-Four*. The fact that the establishment in the BBC could genuinely believe that they were fighting for freedom of speech whilst censoring every word that was uttered over the air and all the while denying (and continuing to deny after the war was over) what they had been doing is one of the finest examples of 'doublethink'.

Dear Mr Rushbrook-Williams,

In confirmation of what I said to you earlier in private, I want to tender my resignation from the BBC and should be much obliged if you would forward this to the proper quarter.

I believe that in speaking to you I made my reasons clear, but I should like to put them on paper lest there should be any mistake. I am not leaving because of any disagreement with BBC policy and still less on account of any kind of grievance. On the contrary I feel that throughout my association with the BBC I have been treated with the greatest generosity and allowed very great latitude. On no occasion have I been compelled to say anything on the air that I would not have said as a private individual. And I should like to take this opportunity of thanking you personally for the very understanding and generous attitude you have always shown towards my work.

I am tendering my resignation because for some time past I have been conscious that I was wasting my own time and the public money on doing work that produces no result. I believe that in the present political situation the broadcasting of British propaganda to India is an almost hopeless task. Whether these broadcasts should be continued at all is for others to judge, but I myself prefer not to spend my time on them when I could be occupying myself with journalism which does produce some measurable effect. I feel that by going back to my normal work of writing and journalism I could be more useful than I am at present.

I do not know how much notice of resignation I am supposed to give. *The Observer* have again raised the project of my going to North Africa. This has to be approved by the War Office and may fall through again but I mention it in case I should have to leave at shorter notice than would otherwise

be the case. I will in any case see to it that the programmes
are arranged for some time ahead.

Yours sincerely,

Eric Blair

The peg on which Orwell hung this letter was that he had been
wasting his time broadcasting to India—not to mention the
Government's money. The day before he resigned, Laurence
Brander had given Orwell a report which showed that what
Orwell said was true, and indeed Orwell got the information
from him. There was one fact he did not add which was that
Brander's researches showed Orwell almost at the bottom in
a list of speakers recognised by the Indian audience. Shortly
before his death Brander cast fresh light on Orwell's position
in the Indian section and this memorandum. Orwell had
raised hackles within the administrative sections of the BBC
as we have seen, but he was also not liked amongst the white
administrators in the Indian section itself, although they
always stood by him. The reason was what was considered
his over-familiarity with the Indian staff. Brander remarked:
'You could see it during the air-raids. We all used to gather in
this room and we always noticed that as groups used to gather
Orwell *always* went and stood with a group of Indians. It was
the same in the pub, he would always surround himself with
Indians which we never did.' The author was able to identify
one of the Indian figures whom Brander never knew the name
of, the editor of *Poetry London*, Tambimuttu, as one of those he
saw Orwell with. Far from being one of the least respected
of the broadcasters in Indian eyes Orwell was the only one
known to be *completely* committed to Indian independence
and was almost a cult figure with them. After the war he
definitely assumed that status to the point where there are
books now circulating in India bearing his name which he
never wrote.

Whether Brander deliberately altered Orwell's position on
the list, or whether, as seemed to be the case in Brander's later

recollections, the respondents to the questionnaire were simply Indians in Delhi in high establishment posts, or even British listeners in India, is not clear. What is certain is that Orwell knew what Brander was going to say and took it as the pretext for writing as he did, knowing it would be unanswerable should any difficulty be made about his resignation. Further, since Brander's report damned the work of the entire department, not just Orwell, it was most unlikely they would make a fuss about his going. What is crystal clear is that the reason he gives, that for some time past he felt he had been wasting his own time and public money, was false. He was leaving because his position had been made impossible through the operation of the censorship system and the politics associated with it over Kingsley Martin and his own talks.

The statements that he had not left because of any grievance and that he had always been treated with 'the greatest generosity' are clearly ironical in the extreme. The cold statement:

> On no occasion have I been compelled to say anything on the air that I would not have said in private life

is as much a justification of his own integrity, preserved against all the odds—how many BBC employees even gave such questions a moment's thought?—than a compliment to the BBC.

On various occasions Orwell praised the BBC as being in general more truthful than the newspapers during the war and was not unsympathetic to those that worked there or the work they were doing. Those who have said that Orwell was satirising the BBC in his creation of the Ministry of Truth in *Nineteen Eighty-Four* cannot have been aware of the role of the Ministry of Information in all Orwell's difficulties at the BBC. There was nothing wrong with the work he did before joining, with Desmond Hawkins for example, and it was this that made work there possible. He was, as he said, given great latitude *on the literary front* and created a blend of programmes using real poets and authors which in many respects foreshadowed

The Third Programme in its best days, and which certainly no longer exists today in Britain.

Between them the Orwells must have had as much knowledge of the real working of the Ministry of Information as any couple in London. The reader will have been able to gather a considerable amount about its activities from this and earlier chapters. It was in fact the central focus of Orwell's great satire.

Lady Mary Blair, daughter of the Earl of Westmorland. The Blairs and the Westmorlands had adjacent estates in Jamaica.
(Courtesy of Mr H.B.B. Dakin)

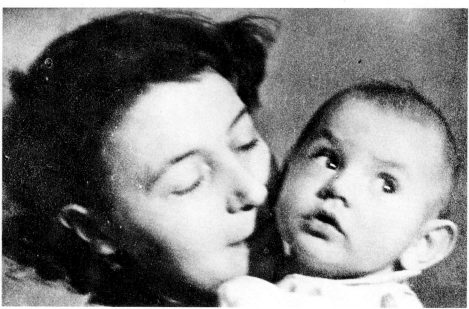

Eileen in North Africa before the war, and *bottom* with Richard Blair at the time she and Orwell decided to go and live on Jura.
(Courtesy of The George Orwell Archive)

Orwell in his flat in Islington, London, shown below his family portrait of Lady Mary Blair. (Courtesy of Mr Vernon Richards)

Senate House, London, by Charles Holden. During the war, this was the headquarters of the Ministry of Information. All censoring systems were co-ordinated
here. Its telegraphic address was 'Miniform'—compare 'Minitrue', that of
Orwell's Ministry of Truth.

THE BOND OF PEACE

THE

BROTHERHOOD

OF

PEACE

J. MIDDLETON MURRY

**THE PEACE PLEDGE UNION
DICK SHEPPARD HOUSE
ENDSLEIGH STREET
LONDON, W.C.1**   3ᴰ·

John Middleton Murry's pamphlet in which he developed the
political idea of 'Brotherhood'. Orwell felt there would
always be a 'Big Brother'.

NOT CHECKED WITH BROADCAST
EASTERN SERVICE
PURPLE NETWORK
Sunday, 17th October, 1943
1515-1545 GMT
GREAT DRAMATISTS No.1.

310 0 5 ~~~~ 16'30" ~~~~

B.B.C.

PASSED FOR SECURITY

DATE.................... SIGNATURE...................

"MACBETH" (15' version)

Production by Hugh Stewart

CAST: Macbeth
        Macduff
        Lady Macbeth
        Doctor
        Seyton
        Young Siward
        Sewart
        Messenger
        Narrator

B.B.C.	
PASSED FOR POLICY	
DATE.................. SIGNATURE..............	

Narrator: We are starting with the great scene early in the play
when Lady Macbeth persuades her only half-willing husband
to murder Duncan. Duncan, King of Scotland, is a guest
at Macbeth's castle. In an earlier scene three witches
have foretold to Macbeth that he himself will one day be
King of Scotland, and the idea of killing Duncan and
seizing the throne has already crossed his mind. Indeed,
he has spoken of it with his wife. But he still shrinks
from the deed; and he is musing alone, half tempted and
half horrified, when Lady Macbeth enters and with a few
skilful speeches nerves him for the murder.

Macbeth: If it were done, when 'tis done, then 'twere well
It were done quickly ....
..........................He's here in double trust;
First, as I am his kinsman, and his subject,
Strong both against the deed; then, as his host,

Orwell's adaptation of *Macbeth* showing the censor's stamps and Orwell's
instruction 'For Censorship Please'. Not even Shakespeare escaped the scrutiny
of the Ministry of Information. (Courtesy of the BBC)

Is This What Our World Is Coming To?

George Orwell

MANY A MAN OR WOMAN, many a parent especially, has said, with a shudder perhaps, "What will our world be like after another generation?" Mr. Orwell's novel describes it as it can be in 1984, and his picture is sometimes breath-taking. It is an account as realistic as if Daniel Defoe had written it, of a society which is like a dreadful machine, where men have no security, where women are taught to hate love, where humor is dead, and the past absolutely wiped out. This is what life *may* be like for our grandchildren, if tendencies luridly visible in the totalitarian states—and present sometimes alarmingly in the democracies—prevail.

¶The scene is England, in a London where even the names have been forgotten of once-famous buildings, now ruined by war. The hero is a plain little fellow, Winston Smith, in blue overalls, the uniform of his party. We follow him into his dirty apartment house where his first act is to turn down—he cannot turn it off—the telescreen, which

(*continued on inside*)

The advance publicity for *Nineteen Eighty-Four*
issued by the book-of-the-month club.

(8(...)) 41352/17l 600m 2/41 M&C Ltd. 706

POSTAL & TELEGRAPH CENSORSHIP. SUBMISSION No. 07/20748/41

P...2'

Terminal Mail ~~Air~~ ~~Surface~~

FO. 20.5.41

C 5691 46

Letter from _Otto Strasser,_ The Windsor Hotel, Montreal, Canada.	To Douglas Reed, C/o Jonathan Cape, Publisher 30, Bedford Square, London, W.C.1.
Address or postmark	MAY 1941
Date of letter or postmark 27.4.41	
	Language German

ORIGINAL LETTER :	SUBMITTED TO :
Submitted............Photographed............	F.O.
Retained............Released....x	INF. DOM
Returned to Sender............	EDITORIAL PRESS M.I.5. Major Rayner.
Seen by : Naval Adviser............Air Adviser............M.I.12............	

SUBJECT

(Include necessary references to Watch Lists, with Authority requiring the Watch)

The following is a translation of a letter from Otto Strasser to his friend Douglas Reed.

"My dear Reed,

I am happy to be able to tell you that we have arrived safely in Canada where I was greeted by your nice letter, for which many thanks.

In the short time since our arrival I have been very busy — first 5 days in Montreal, then 3 in Ottawa, then 8 in Toronto, then yesterday again in Montreal, where we are going to stay for the present. After all these talks I have come to the conclusion that Canada is a good hunting ground and that I can hope for understanding and assistance. I was especially successful in my interview with Mr. John Stevenson, editor of the "Globe and Mail" and correspondent for the London "Times". He not only arranged a whole lot of valuable interviews, but also a "Stop Press Interview" that took place on the evening of the 25th in Toronto. (After which was a really good press conference,)

Operating Unit	Section	Examiner	D.A.C.	Date
	PO/PMS	472		15.5.41.

Postal Censorship report on a letter sent to the publisher Jonathan Cape.
All publishers were on the watch lists and detailed files on their activities were
kept by MI5—see their name on the circulation list here. (Courtesy of HMSO)

CHAPTER EIGHT

The Ministry of Truth

L ooking south-east from Langford Court, built on high ground in London's St John's Wood, one building stood clear of all others; it was the tallest building in London apart from St Paul's Cathedral, the Ministry of Information building in Bloomsbury. Designed by the architect Charles Holden as the central administrative building of the University of London, it symbolised the new world of the meritocracy in architecture which resembled similar buildings in the Soviet Union. In describing it as the Ministry of Truth building in *Nineteen Eighty-Four*, Orwell exaggerated its height somewhat but the effect was the same. It towered over the Georgian buildings in Bloomsbury exactly as he describes it. It resembled nothing so much as the well-known proposals for the Palace of the Soviets in Moscow which was to be crowned by a statue of Stalin—in *Nineteen Eighty-Four* the statue of Big Brother is more appropriately placed on the top of Nelson—sorry, Big Brother's column in Trafalgar—sorry, Victory Square.

A Ministry of Information had existed in the First World War and its final importance in the propaganda war had been so great that it was realised, with the arrival of the new media of radio and television, that something would have to be in place the moment war was declared to produce the strongest propaganda from the first shot. It would have to concern itself not just with the dissemination of information—news was only one aspect of this—but also keep a strict watch on the content of the news and everything the people of Britain said or did that might be of any use to the enemy. It was for this reason that the censorship of the mails, although carried out by the Post Office was funded on the Ministry of Information budget. The bureaucratic apparatus that gathered together in the Ministry of Information building—telegraphic address *Miniform*, compare the newspeak word for the Ministry of Truth *Minitrue*—was potentially an instrument of totalitarian power as threatening as anything seen in the actual totalitarian states in Europe.

The reason the MOI had these overtones was of course because it not only created news and information it censored it. We have seen the Orwells' experience of this work of the MOI from two different perspectives, Eileen's as censor and Orwell's as both writer and producer; it is now necessary to look closely at the thing itself. Orwell gave an admirable description of what the Ministry of Information did in *Nineteen Eighty-Four*:

> The Ministry of Truth['s] primary job was . . . to supply the citizens of Oceania with newspapers, films, textbooks, telescreen programmes, plays, novels—with every conceivable kind of information, instruction or entertainment . . .

Television had actually stopped the day war began but apart from that the satire was very accurate. The MOI's most public face was seen by the press, usually foreign papers including the then neutral United States of America. They would come to file their stories and watch as a clerk put them into a container and sent them down a pneumatic tube to the censors working invisibly somewhere else in the building. After a time the container would reappear with the story either passed or blue-pencilled by someone it was never possible to speak to who was working to a set of rules it was never possible to query, some anonymous party member receiving material for papers around the world, and sending it back rewritten to comply with the truth, just as Winston Smith does in *Nineteen Eighty-Four*.

The person in charge of the press censors was the Controller of Press and Censorship, Francis Williams, a left-wing journalist who before the war had worked as editor of the *Daily Herald*. At the head of the ministry was the close confidant of Winston Churchill, the Minister of Information, Brendan Bracken, known throughout the ministry as B.B.

There were serious tasks for the censors, of course, and Orwell knew this as well as anyone. The leaking of military secrets was the thing most to be avoided. There was a classic example of this in the hours leading up to D-Day, the invasion of Europe. Secrecy was absolutely paramount both about the time of the invasion and the location, and yet, two days before Eisenhower's troops began their landings, a telegram was sent out on the Associated Press wire saying the invasion had begun. It was noticed immediately that the message 'URGENT PRESS ASSOCIATED UK. FLASH. EISENHOWER'S HEADQUARTERS ANNOUNCE ALLIED LANDING' did not have the initials PBC (Passed by Censor) before and after it, nor a correct code number. Immediately a cancellation message was sent out but it was too late and several radio stations around the world broke into their programmes to announce that the invasion of Europe had begun. Investigation established that the break in security had been caused by a young cipher clerk who had been practising the signal that was due to go out and had inadvertently left the words on a tape used to send another message. In the event the German intelligence took this as being part of a war of nerves, as they no doubt saw for themselves that there was no censor's code on the message.

Orwell had sent many scripts off to be censored in just this way, more than he cared to remember no doubt, and would have seen nothing wrong with this at all. But there were other aspects of censorship which can be seen operating, for example, in the film industry.

The MOI not only published books and pamphlets in immense numbers, they also had film teams that put together documentaries to be shown in cinemas around the country and abroad. A wide variety of people were used to produce them and the MOI files record that Inez Holden wrote the script of one on work in factories, the kind of work she and Orwell's sister Avril had actually been doing. The MOI's concern with films did not stop there. They needed to know exactly which ones were going to be shown to the British public by private film companies and the effect they would have. In order to get advance warning of the American films coming into Britain, which were the majority of films watched by the public, the MOI censors copied all telegrammes from Hollywood and New York to the Cinema department which was run by Jack Beddington. So prolific were the Hollywood men in their use of telegrammes that when the censorship of telegrammes was being wound down at the end of the war it was found that Beddington's intercepts accounted for two thirds of all those on the censors' watch lists. It is clear that Beddington, who was a central figure in the Cafe Royal set, made good use of the information he obtained in this way. The MOI, for its part, was able to determine well in advance which productions were likely to cause it trouble.

When it came to dealing with the films themselves brought into the MOI there were very well equipped film and photographic studios which Francis Williams later described with great pride. Moving film was readily censored by cutting anything deemed 'difficult'. With still photographs the situation could often be remedied by 'touching up' the images using a variety of sophisticated techniques. It was soon discovered that when these touched up photographs were sent out over the wires it was almost impossible to tell that there had been any interference with the image at all. Williams was particularly proud of these studios which had been set up in order to avoid having to use the commercial photographers who had done similar work before the war for the advertising agencies. They were used initially but security considerations made this undesirable. The MOI also had typography experts who could duplicate any typeface that might be needed for agents working in Germany or France or to create propaganda material to be dropped by air or sent by post. Again Orwell's *Nineteen Eighty-Four* sums up the atmosphere:

> Beyond, above, below were other swarms of workers engaged in an unimaginable multitude of jobs. There were the huge printing shops with their sub-editors, their typography experts and their elaborately equipped studios for the faking of photographs.

It may be asked how Orwell could have known that such secret work was being carried out, and whether it was more likely that he was creating a world out of elements he had known in Spain and elsewhere rather than satirising the MOI. There are clear indications of his knowledge to be found in his BBC work. In particular he commissioned a programme from Ritchie Calder on the subject of microfilms in September 1942 asking him not to be too technical and to:

> . . . establish in the first few minutes just what microfilms are as it is certain that some of your readers will never have heard of them. I should like the important part that these things are likely to play in preventing libraries from being destroyed by bombs or by the police of totalitarian regimes to be emphasised.

Orwell knew Ritchie Calder well and had commissioned his book *The Lesson of London* for the Searchlight Books series he had edited with Tosco Fyvel. And Calder was very knowledgable about films and the latest advances at the MOI, no doubt in part because he shared a flat in London with Francis Williams. Orwell knew little or nothing about such things as microfilms and was asking Calder to speak on what he had already learnt from Calder and found worth a programme.

A key element in the MOI's make-up was how the policy which the censors used was actually arrived at, and who implemented it. The range of issues was vast covering every kind of domestic and international issue, as well as the on-going daily coverage of the war itself. An easy way into the labyrinthine paths that the 'truth' followed before it reached the world is to look at what happened to the ministers of each ministry when they spoke to the world, from the Prime Minister downwards.

Even Churchill was once censored. Talking to Roosevelt on the transatlantic telephone, he was discussing matters of high policy when a censor's voice cut in to tell him that he could not mention such matters and that if he continued he would have no option but to cut him off. This little difficulty took a few moments to resolve and no doubt provided some much wanted humour to lighten a dark hour in Anglo-American affairs. Churchill was fully conscious of the dangers of uncoordinated talks by his ministers and took special care to see that ministers did not speak out of turn over the radio. The well-known speakers' procedure which we have seen used by Orwell at the BBC was followed in the case of ministers except that the talks used were cleared by a special procedure which was kept extremely secret.

The MOI liaison with the BBC was close and usually censors' instructions were sent to the BBC in telegrammes written in a language which closely resembled that used by O'Brien in *Nineteen Eighty-Four*. Ministers' talks were not subjected to the usual censorship within the BBC but sent over to the MOI. They would eventually return with the censors' stamps on them. What happened within the MOI remained a mystery. In fact they were taken to Brendan Bracken who in turn gave them to Churchill and he actually 'censored' them himself. The war cabinet was exempt from this procedure, but this was simply because Churchill would already know of any planned broadcast at this level. On one occasion he telephoned a cabinet minister at the microphone in the studio prior to broadcasting to dictate a suitable passage for inclusion. On at least two other occasions he banned a minister's talk entirely, not leaving it at that but moving the minister concerned to another post. These were talks by Harold Nicolson and R. A. Butler. Nicolson made the mistake of saying in his talk that the Members of Parliament would put up with much but they would never agree to shout out *'Heil* Churchill!'. Churchill responded by removing Nicolson from his post, no less than Parliamentary Under Secretary to the Minister of Information, to a governorship of the BBC. R. A. Butler submitted a talk that was so deeply depressing that it ended up by saying there was no real hope for the future of the country except the education of Britain's youth to keep alive the principles of freedom. Churchill responded by sending Butler to the Ministry of Education where in due course he produced the 1944 Education Act. Both talks remained on file at the BBC, unbroadcast.

Policy for each ministry, at this level, was simply that set by Churchill. At the next level down policy was set by the senior officials of each ministry all of whom had desks at the MOI. There were in addition 'desks' that dealt with a wide range of affairs such as the Russian desk which liased with the Soviet embassy when Russia entered the war upon invasion by Germany. It was in these areas that the possibility of political action and infiltration became acute. Orwell was well aware of this but quite probably never put his finger on exactly how pressure was brought to bear, although he felt the pressure acutely as we have seen. It was the MOI Russian desk that logged the first complaint about Orwell's anti-Stalin news broadcast. How they knew is not clear, but if it was a leak within the BBC then Burgess would have been the obvious suspect—he was a close personal friend of the man at the Russian desk who is now thought to have also been a Soviet agent, Peter Smollett.

It is worth emphasising here the great difference between the kind of censorship which prevented such mistakes as the leaking of an invasion date and the political censorship which emanated from such departments as the Russian desk at the MOI. Orwell made the point quite clearly in his satire:

What happened in the unseen labyrinth to which the pneumatic tubes led, he did not know in detail, but he

did know in general terms . . . [the] process of continual
alteration was applied not only to newspapers but to books,
periodicals, pamphlets . . . sound-tracks, cartoons, photographs—to every kind of literature or documentation which
might conceivably hold any *political or ideological significance.*
[emphasis added]

It was the monitoring of books, periodicals and pamphlets
which most worried Orwell and which were so close to the
activities of the totalitarian powers themselves that those
responsible for carrying out this work had to develop standards
which were admirably described by Orwell as 'doublethink'.
The undoubted existence within Britain of groups ideologically
opposed to the war provided a useful starting point for those
who wished to justify the disruption of the tradition of free
speech which had survived in Britain across the centuries after
the most bitter struggles. But they kept their justification to
themselves and the public remained in complete ignorance of
what went on, or how this intrusion was carried out.

In 1944 Orwell attacked the role of literary censor which the
MOI was increasingly assuming. Having first mentioned the
way the press could be muzzled in peace time, as it had over
the case of Mrs Simpson and the Prince of Wales, he went on
to describe what had been happening during the war:

Nowadays this kind of veiled censorship even extends to
books. The MOI does not, of course, dictate a party line or
issue an *Index Expurgatorius*. It merely "advises". Publishers
take manuscripts to the MOI and the MOI "suggests" that
this or that is undesirable, or premature or "would serve no
good purpose". And though there is no definite prohibition,
no clear statement that this or that may not be printed, official
policy is never flouted.

Later writers have taken this account literally, without realising
that it simply took to the limit what could be said in print at
the time without being banned by the censor. Had Orwell said

anything more he would have broken one of the D notices and that issue of *Tribune* would have been suppressed. The pointers are his use of direct quotation clearly from a letter in his possession and the tell-tale 'of course'.

It is true that in the very narrow world of London publishing a hint was often all that was necessary. But the first question was how the hint came to be delivered, how, indeed, the MOI knew of books in advance, as it often did. The answer was, once again, the censorship system. All publishers were on the watch list used by the telegramme censors, alongside the cinema companies. Since the first step a publisher or agent took when they had a book which was in any sense live or controversial was to try to sell American rights the MOI knew from that moment that the book existed. Orwell's name was already well known to the censors through his column in *Partisan Review*. Others were in a similar position and also had their files that kept careful track of everything they did. It did not need many friendly hints from officials for publishers to realise that certain authors were 'doubtful' and that the correct position would be to send the script in for comment. The same system operates today and it is a brave publisher that will not send a book to the secretary of the D notice committee when he writes suggesting it might be a good idea, although strictly speaking there is no compulsion to do so.

The exact procedure that was followed for each text is not clear, despite the papers that have been released, and Francis Williams' own writing which speaks quite candidly of his frequent conversations with MI5 officers, although only specifically with reference to German spies. What is clear is that when texts were suppressed this was very frequently for ideological reasons and not security ones. It is obvious that if any novel gave a detailed and accurate account, for example, of Britain's black broadcasting operations then it would be called in on security grounds alone. But this was the exception. The books and pamphlets that were called in were looked upon much as the inquisition might have looked upon heretical texts, or a seventeenth-century puritan any recusant text or play. With virtually all the Mosleyite pamphleteers either detained without trial or cowed into silence the only ideological enemies to hand were those picked out by such as the Soviet desk of the MOI. They had a wealth of enemies and Orwell was an almost classic example of one of them from his days with the POUM to his activities at the time of the People's Convention.

The situation at the MOI was not static. In its early days there had been much criticism of its amateurishness; Evelyn Waugh and others have given fictional accounts of life there. The arrival of B.B. changed all that and kept things on an even keel whilst the worst news Britain ever had to hear was dealt with as even-handedly and skilfully as possible. However with the invasion of North Africa and the beginning of the fight back in Europe things changed again. The MOI which took the Soviet line was not following one which Churchill would have agreed with and Brendan Bracken shared his views. Inevitably divisions within the Ministry appeared with 'reconstruction' being used as a code word much repeated by those who looked for drastic changes when the war was over. The campaign in Greece, when a communist uprising was put down, exposed the ideological divisions within the MOI. Churchill ensured that his view was the one that prevailed but within the MOI the official 'line' could vary from its agents in the field, and at one point the MOI was pro-communist when British troops were actually fighting the Greek communists. Francis Williams was well aware of the situation, as the person responsible for the decision on whether to censor or not. His published memoirs are silent on the struggles that went on within the MOI but an occasional remark betrays his knowledge:

> Burgess [I knew] quite well during his time at the Foreign Office News Division at the Ministry of Information and later when he was personal assistant to my friend Hector McNeil . . .

He had earlier written of him:

No one had any reason to question this appointment [of Philby] at that time, any more than I or anyone else had reason to suspect a loud drunken member of the Foreign Office News Division at the MOI, Guy Burgess, of being anything but an occasional public nuisance.

The slight contradiction between these two statements conceals a very great gulf between what Francis Williams knew and what he was prepared to say. And the key fact that reveals this gulf is that Burgess took the pro-Soviet line in any policy dispute within the MOI, and Williams knew this, indeed could not help but know it when affairs such as the policy on Greece caused conflict between the MOI and the government. There were others besides Burgess of course, but it was only he who, in the end, took the courage of his convictions to the point where he actually defected, revealing exactly what had been going on in the BBC and the MOI.

The censorship of literary texts written in England was approached by the MOI in a spirit little different from that of the seventeenth-century puritans so it is perhaps appropriate that one of the few works which actually appeared to justify their existence should be a political fable, written on one level for children, with the disarming title of *Animal Farm*.

CHAPTER NINE

Animal Farm

When Orwell left the BBC it was with a feeling of intense relief, tinged with some disappointment. The bureaucracy and political infighting were behind him, but he had not been able to get the job he most wanted, that of political correspondent of the *Observer* for the North African campaign. As he suspected, his health was not good enough; he shrewdly remarked this would have meant the paper or the army would have had to have paid Eileen a pension if he had not returned. However he did not leave without a job to go to. When he failed the medical Tosco Fyvel took soundings on his behalf and discovered that the post of Literary Editor of *Tribune* would soon become available. Jon Kimche then the Literary Editor was a mutual friend of Orwell and Fyvel and there was no problem. The duties were onerous but only kept Orwell in the office three days a week whilst the pay at £500 was only marginally less than he had been getting at the BBC, and a good amount in those days. Orwell's reputation for presenting such programmes as 'Voice' stood him in good stead, for there can have been few poetry editors who were so well connected at the time, from T. S. Eliot to the latest 'Apocalyptic' poets.

What Orwell wanted most of all was the time which the BBC had not allowed him. It was not simply the work there, but the immense amount of bureaucratic struggle with its hard-to-follow political overtones, not to mention the back-stabbing activities of people such as Guy Burgess who professed open friendship. It is hardly surprising that he soon filled the time available with work of his own, at last, and produced his first fiction since the fragmentary *Story by Five Authors*, and his adaptations of others' work, such as *The Fox*. There is even a possibility that the story of *Animal Farm* was actually conceived as a radio play. Orwell did a radio version of it which shows some signs of taking precedence over the prose version. For example when Mollie has asked if there will be sugar after the Rebellion Napoleon replies, in the radio version:

No, certainly not. When we are in control of this farm it will have to be self supporting. We have no means of making sugar here.

The published version has Napoleon saying in answer:

No, we have no means of making sugar on this farm.

It seems that the published text is an edited version of the radio script rather than the other way around, and this does suggest that at least Orwell was working from a body of material for *Animal Farm* which was created before the final prose version.

In 1946, shortly after the publication of *Animal Farm*, Orwell wrote:

Animal Farm was the first book in which I tried with full consciousness of what I was doing, to fuse political purpose and artistic purpose into one whole. I have not written a novel for seven years, but I hope to write another fairly soon. It is bound to be a failure, every book is a failure, but I know with some clarity what kind of book I want to write.

This remarkable statement shows that his experience at the BBC had not beaten him down. Rather he set to work on *Animal Farm* with clarity of purpose, that same clarity with which he was contemplating writing *Nineteen Eighty-Four*. His political purpose was to expose the dangers if Stalin's communism or anything like it appeared in Britain. His artistic purpose is less easy to describe if only because *Animal Farm* differs so completely from everything which he had written before. Writing a preface for the book in 1947 he made it quite clear that he had had the idea for the book six years before when living in Wallington. He had seen a large cart horse being driven along by a ten-year-old boy and had thought that if only the cart horse could realise the strength he had the position would be different. This is the political idea, developed through a study of the history of the revolution in Russia as it actually happened. The artistic background perhaps begins at this time also. Silone's *The Fox* was first published by John Lehman at the time Orwell said he got the original idea. It was in a magazine to which Orwell also contributed, and which he cannot have helped seeing. The stories Orwell chose to adapt were ones he thought particularly good and if he had only just come across it in 1943 it is less likely he would have responded so positively. Also, during the war he began to think about children's stories for the very practical reason that, whilst he did not have any children of his own he was godfather to Mulk Raj Anand's daughter, and many of his friends also had children. Herbert Read made a point of saying in his letter about *Animal Farm* that he had read it to his son:

> He has insisted on my reading, chapter by chapter, every evening since, and he enjoys it innocently as much as I enjoy it maliciously. It thus stands the test that only classics of satire like *Gulliver* survive.

The blurb on the dust jacket of *Animal Farm*, probably written by Roger Senhouse, also refers to Swift:

> In this good natured satire upon dictatorship George Orwell makes use of the technique perfected by Swift in *Tale of a Tub*.

Senhouse wrote a similarly misleading blurb for *Nineteen Eighty-Four* as we shall see—Orwell was not good natured when it came to the dangers of Stalinism—but the acknowledgement to Swift is genuine enough.

It is clear that Orwell wished his message to reach as many people as possible and last as long as possible and the form of a fairy story aimed at children chimed in with those aims. T. S. Eliot wrote his poems about cats for the children of his friend Geoffrey Tandy, who also suggested they be broadcast, and Eliot's friends were as surprised as Orwell's at the new side to his character that was revealed. There was one other element which the Orwells' friends were aware of, which Orwell made no secret of, and that was the role Eileen played in writing the book. Writing to Max Plowman's widow he lamented that Eileen had died before the book appeared and that this was particularly sad as she had helped to plan it.

Eileen's influence has been mentioned by many writers, including Orwell's biographers, but what possible form her help could have taken has not been discussed. There are two pointers to the likely nature of this help. First, before Eileen married Orwell she had run a secretarial bureau. However this seems to have been of a very specialised kind, for surviving books from her library in the Orwell archive collection include at least one from a grateful author for the work she did on his book. In fact she appears to have ghosted the book. Colleagues of hers at the time have described a similar instance where she effectively rewrote a thesis that someone asked the agency to type. Secondly, after leaving the Censorship Department she worked for the Ministry of Food doing radio programmes for housewives giving them menus and cooking hints which they could use within the rationing system. She even did a broadcast for Orwell's own Indian station. Orwell referred to their marriage as being a real one where they shared worries and struggles, and, at least as far as work went, they certainly did. As we have already seen their shared knowledge of the censorship systems and the political and ideological struggles in the BBC was substantial. She never showed signs of wanting to be a writer herself but in *Animal Farm* got very close to it, frequently telling her friends in the Ministry exactly how she and Orwell were getting along. Orwell himself seems never to have talked of work in progress.

In the first full-scale biography of Orwell, Bernard Crick suggested that *Animal Farm* and *Nineteen Eighty-Four* were much more closely related than they at first seemed and that there were actually close resemblances which critics had failed to notice, particularly in their origin. This he found in the projected three-volume family saga, provisionally called *The Quick and the Dead*, which Orwell had said he was writing in a questionnaire he filled in for an American magazine in 1940. The suggestion is convincing, and is based on the direct evidence of a notebook which has survived in the Orwell archive which contains notes for *The Quick and the Dead* but then continues with the first outlines of *Nineteen Eighty-Four*. The one convincing detail that carries over from the earlier project to *Animal Farm* is the horse, Boxer. No longer the horse being driven along a country lane, he is one being driven almost to its death by an army officer, but the idea is clearly still there. The original form of a family saga was simply a continuation of the kind of novel he was writing before the war, notably *Coming up for Air*, with a wider perspective across the generations, no doubt suggested by the death of his father in 1939.

The experience of the war, so different from what he expected, completely changed his ideas. Had he gone into uniform immediately and fought against fascism as he had done in Spain no doubt he would have come home at the end to write some saga of the kind he thought of in 1940. (The resemblance between the title of his proposed book and Norman Mailer's *The Naked and the Dead* is completely coincidental but none the less uncanny for that). The war instead proved to be one of privation and propaganda and, as it ended, an unpleasant echo of the political struggles at the end of the Spanish civil war. Boxer survived in *Animal Farm* still the same essential beast of burden that he had been all along in Orwell's imagination. The pig Napoleon surely derives from

Silone's pig Benito as a literary idea, as does the actual form of the book.

Of the millions of people who have read *Animal Farm* barely a handful can have followed the political parallels exactly. Many more have taken it in the spirit in which Herbert Read read it to his son rather than in that of a pointed political satire, which was how Orwell saw it. Clearly it *is* a political satire, written with Swift as an original inspiration—Silone would have meant nothing to those reading Senhouse's original blurb—but the detail could only be followed by someone with a good knowledge of the politics of the time. A clear instance of this can be found at the end of the preface which he wrote for the Ukrainian edition of *Animal Farm*:

> A number of readers may finish the book with the impression that it ends in the complete reconciliation of the pigs and humans. That was not my intention; on the contrary I meant it to end on a loud note of discord, for I wrote it immediately after the Tehran Conference which everybody thought had established the best possible relations between the USSR and the West. I personally did not believe that such good relations would last long; and, as events have shown, I wasn't far wrong . . .

The most interesting thing about this reference to the Tehran Conference, an event which not one reader of *Animal Farm* in a hundred thousand would have heard of either at the time the book came out or later, is that in a letter to Roger Senhouse he pointed to the same origin for *Nineteen Eighty-Four*:

> What it is really meant to do is to discuss the implications of dividing the world up into 'Zones of influence' (I thought of it in 1944 as a result of the Tehran Conference), and to indicate by parodying them the intellectual implications of totalitarianism.

1944 is possibly a slip for 1943, as this is mentioned in another letter to his publisher Fred Warburg, and also from the fact that the Tehran Conference was in 1943. This detail confirms Crick's hypothesis that the two books are closely related, for who could imagine from reading them that the author thought both sprang at least in part from the same event.

The most direct evidence of the connection between the two books is that at the time he was writing *Animal Farm* he also drafted a first outline of the book he called *The Last Man in Europe* which eventually became *Nineteen Eighty-Four*. When this outline first appeared in print, as an appendix to Professor Crick's biography of Orwell, the existence of Orwell's BBC texts was not known, nor was the exact significance of the job Eileen held in the Censorship Department. It can now be seen that the book which we know as *Nineteen Eighty-Four* stemmed directly from Orwell's experience at the BBC, or the war—Miniform and the rest—as seen from the perspective of the BBC, backed up by his wife's knowledge. Brief though they are the immediate influence is seen in such entries in the outline as 'Enemy Propaganda and the writer's response to it' and 'Effects of lies and hatred produced by: . . . Broadcasts'. And the first three sections of Part 1 can be taken as an obvious expression of the revulsion he felt at the systematised lying to the people which formed the heart of the BBC's position when under the control of the Ministry of Information.

Orwell's feeling that most of his colleagues were engaged in what was little more than lying is obvious from incidents such as his response to a request for a talk from a Home Service producer after he had left the BBC. Orwell replied that he would be happy to do something provided he did not have to say anything untruthful. There was no reply, and no offer of a programme; doubtless the producer was insulted, or thought Orwell an obvious source of trouble. What cannot be in doubt is that Orwell thought that truth and truthfulness was the first thing to be mentioned. In modern terms someone responding in this way would be said to be 'paranoid'. However, as we have seen, there was indeed systematised lying and general acceptance of behaviour, such as the circulation of opened mail in transit, which was at the same time said to be exactly the thing being fought against. It is always the 'left' which makes play with such ideas as 'paranoia' and it is no coincidence that it was in Soviet Russia that people, including writers, were habitually placed in asylums for the insane if they disagreed with party orthodoxy.

In some ways the 1943 outline of *Nineteen Eighty-Four* looks more like one of the earlier Orwell books. The central character of the writer is still obviously a projection of Orwell himself, and a similar figure appears in most of his books. The book that finally appeared had lost that element. Winston Smith can hardly be called a writer, simply a semi-literate person, barely capable of writing, who starts a diary. The diary is present in this first draft, and then the idea that it would be continued mentally—not present in the final version—which would lead finally to Winston's madness. Orwell clearly felt completely isolated when he left the BBC, to be able to contemplate such a book.

The setting of the book in the future is seen in the 1943 draft from the confusion of events which were thought to have happened in the seventies, then sometime in the past. We have seen his series 'A.D. 2000' and, for any indication to the contrary, he might have been intending to set his book at some time like that looking back on revolutionary events which had happened in 1974, just as he was looking back on real revolutionary events which had happened in 1917 from the perspective of 1944. The idea of looking at events in the future from some date even further off derives directly from Jack London and *The Iron Heel*, as do several other ideas present in this outline and also in the final book.

Orwell's interest in Jack London can be followed in a series of essays. The first was published in *Tribune* in July 1940. He made an interesting passing reference in his essay 'Wells, Hitler and the World State' in *Horizon* in August 1941, then there was a broadcast on London on 5 March, 1943 and a further article in *Tribune* on 30 June, 1944. He went on to make further references, but at this time it is possible to see a development in the influence London had, and in particular *The Iron Heel*. In his 1944 essay he remarked:

> About a year ago I had to do a broadcast on Jack London. When I started to collect the material I found that those of his books that I most wanted had vanished so completely that even the London Library could not produce them . . . this seems to me a disaster for Jack London is one of those borderline writers whose work might be forgotten unless somebody takes the trouble to revive them. Even *The Iron Heel* was distinctly a rarity for some years, and it was only reprinted because Hitler's rise to power made it topical . . .

It is interesting to see that although Orwell reviewed the reprint of *The Iron Heel* in 1940 (the essay in Tribune was a review of this) he did not pursue London seriously as an author until he was moved to do so for his radio talk in March 1943. In the 1940 essay, 'Prophecies of Fascism', which we noticed in an earlier chapter, he does compare *The Iron Heel* with Huxley's *Brave New World*, and Wells' *The Sleeper Wakes*, but only in terms of its success or failure as a prophecy. In the 1941 essay he remarks, again *a propos* of Wells:

> A crude book like *The Iron Heel*, written nearly thirty years ago, is a truer prophecy of the future than either *Brave New World* or *The Shape of Things to Come*.

A firmer judgement but again there is no sign that he was himself looking at writing that kind of book. His broadcast essay on London is something quite different and there are very clear signs of his thinking on the same lines as his final book. He does not merely talk in general terms about the book being a prophecy of the future, but about the book's political purpose:

> It is a curious fact that London's own political writings have almost escaped attention in his own country and Britain. Ten

or fifteen years ago when *The Iron Heel* was widely read and admired in France and Germany, it was out of print and almost unobtainable in Britain, and even now, though an English edition of it exists, few people have heard of it.

The broadcast was short and Orwell apologised for not being able to talk about London's other political and sociological writings. However he identified a key element in London's books from which their validity sprang and that was his perception that 'hedonistic societies cannot endure, a perception that isn't common amongst what are called progressive thinkers'.

As we shall see Orwell's vision of gloom developed after the end of the war and other elements were added to the outline, but the central features stemming from Jack London's work still remain. The idea of the proles—that is a Jack London word found in *The Iron Heel*—and talk of the relationship between the parties and the trusts all stem from London. The point is of interest because from quite early on it has been suggested that Orwell got his ideas from another writer Zamyatin, and, more than that, that his entire book was in some direct sense a plagiarism. Writing to Gleb Struve on 17 February 1944, to thank him for a copy of his book 25 *Years of Soviet Russian Literature*, he said:

> It has already roused my interest in Zamyatin's *We*, which I had not heard of before. I am interested in that kind of book, and even keep making notes for one myself that may get written sooner or later . . . I am writing a little squib which might amuse you when it comes out, but it is not so O.K. politically that I don't feel certain in advance that anyone will publish it. Perhaps that gives you a hint of its subject.

The 'squib' was of course *Animal Farm* and the fortunate survival of this letter shows us the two books appearing together, and the unquestionable fact that Zamyatin's *We* was new to Orwell at the time and he cannot have been led to write his book or even the 1943 outline by it. In fact, interestingly enough, Zamyatin is in many respects properly considered as an *English* author like Conrad, much influenced by H. G. Wells, as was Orwell. But Orwell had moved on from there.

The reference to the making of notes for *Nineteen Eighty-Four* in his letter to Struve rings true, for it is obvious that the imaginative ideas that appear in the outline—Newspeak, the party slogans 'War is Peace. Ignorance is Strength. Freedom is Slavery.', Eurasia, East Asia (still two separate words at this stage) and so on—did not appear all at once. He must have known clearly what he meant by Newspeak, and what underlay the slogans when he wrote the outline. The reference in his March 1943 talk to London's political ideas, combined with his later reference to political purpose in his writing of *Animal Farm* (and by implication *Nineteen Eighty-Four* started but not finished then), suggests that the notes first began at about that time. Orwell's series 'A.D. 2000' began in June 1942, and his proposal to include a talk on Jack London was first made in December 1942. Without any direct information in the form of other letters or journals which may still await discovery this is probably as far as this kind of speculation can be taken. It is nonetheless of great importance in analysing the influence of the world of the Miniform controlled BBC on Orwell's creative imagination, the change from the Orwell who could project a family saga of a literary kind and the Orwell of *Animal Farm* and *Nineteen Eighty-Four*.

There was one further valid point Orwell made in his letter to Gleb Struve and that was that he might have trouble getting *Animal Farm* published. That proved an understatement, but the interesting angle is that he realised that he would have difficulty because it was 'Not so OK *politically*'.

CHAPTER TEN

Wartime Literary Censorship in Britain

Freedom of speech in wartime has to be conditional for obvious reasons. We have seen that intrusion into this fundamental democratic right in Britain in the 1939–45 war extended right through to the opening of all private mail going abroad (and a considerable quantity of internal mail), the monitoring of everything that appeared in the newspapers and of all political movements, with penalties under emergency powers legislation including detention without trial. However draconian these powers may have seemed from a peacetime perspective they were necessary if the country was to survive the first real threat of invasion since Napoleonic times; Orwell supported most of them in practice and a lot in theory whilst uttering warnings. However he did not go the final stage and agree with the censorship of literature itself, and neither did the Government, officially. Fundamental freedoms of this kind were very close indeed to what was being fought for. The official in the censorship department who said that if it was ever found out what they had been doing they would be called the English Gestapo was voicing a real fear and also giving a fine example of Orwell's 'system of organised lying' as he put it in the first *Nineteen Eighty-Four* outline.

The cornerstone of any system which censors literary work is the compliance of the publishers, even in wartime. The totalitarian way is, on the face of things, not the English way or at least it had not been until the twentieth century saw

105

the overthrowing of so many of Britain's hard-won freedoms. There has to be something like a consensus amongst leading figures in what later came to be called the establishment which agrees, within fairly wide boundaries, that something like the censorship of literature should take place. In Britain the Committee which dealt with censorship, the Press and Censorship Bureau of the Ministry of Information, the D-notice committee as it is presently called, had sitting on it members of the various publishers' professional bodies and some publishers themselves. In fact this committee seems hardly to have met in wartime as Sir Stanley Unwin who represented the Publishers Association revealed in his memoirs:

> [My services] were never required. In doubtful cases publishers voluntarily and gladly submitted typescripts or proofs, and the censors dealt with them expeditiously. The expression of opinions remained free.

Professor Crick, citing this passage remarked 'Here is double-think indeed', and rightly so. It is the existence of men who were capable of holding two such thoughts in their heads at the same time—expression of opinion remained free, and yet all doubtful scripts were voluntarily submitted for censorship—that enabled the totalitarian system of thought and practice to take root in Britain. And it took root not just in the security services but in the minds of all who had a 'need to know' what was going on, in the MOI, the BBC, and a hundred other departments elsewhere—the establishment. Burgess in one of his more lucid BBC memoranda referred to the system as 'bureaucratic totalitarianism'; it was the central target of Orwell's most savage attacks in *Nineteen Eighty-Four*.

As Orwell died at such an early age, before 'freedom of information' was even an idea, before even Burgess had defected, it is doubtful whether he ever knew exactly the sort of battle he had been fighting, or how the censorship that he fell foul of actually worked. It is now possible to draw some firm conclusions freed from the taint of accusations of 'paranoia' and witch-hunting that for long prevailed. It is worth remembering, again, that at the time Orwell died any suggestion that, for example, Burgess was a Soviet agent would have been taken as pure malice and sure sign of what would have been called then a 'mania'; talking about censorship would have been called a 'persecution complex'. But the facts were that Burgess and his colleagues, known as Stalin's Englishmen, *were* spies and Orwell *was* the victim of censorship on a large scale.

Orwell's suggestion in his letter to Gleb Struve that his book was 'not so OK politically' that he could be sure of finding a publisher shows that he was aware that there might be a problem, but not that he knew exactly how the system operated. Before looking in detail at the banning of *Animal Farm* it is necessary to look at other works by Orwell which were either banned or delayed at this time. Some examples which involved simple censorship or deletions have been mentioned already and there were many more no doubt. Here we list only books which were actually banned or suspended, that is completely censored.

1. A review of Harold Laski's *Faith Reason and Civilisation* due to appear 16 March, 1944. Banned.
2. *Animal Farm* first submitted to publisher 19 March 1944 published on 17 August, 1945.
3. *The English People*. Finished and submitted to publisher May 1944; not published until 1947.
4. 'Propaganda and Demotic Speech'. Written April 1944 and publication delayed until summer 1944.
5. 'Some notes on Salvador Dali'. Written in June 1944 for the *Saturday Book*. Actually printed and bound before being physically removed from the book and an alternative text by another author inserted in its place.

Close examination of Orwell's work will reveal other possible delays and interferences, but these are clear and firm examples all of which date from 1944.

It might seem at first that there is an element of chance here and that if *Animal Farm* triggered the ban then why was the Laski review stopped before Orwell sent the text off? However there are two possible explanations which between them make it clear that a ban was in place whatever the exact mechanism. First, from the discovery of the BBC material and the way the Censorship Department worked, described here for the first time, it is clear that Orwell had an MOI file, and that he had been involved in a series of bitter censorship struggles at the BBC over figures as important as Kingsley Martin and J.B.S. Haldane, besides his own scripts. All these incidents would have been written up in full on his file at the MOI, and also, no doubt, copied over to MI5. That the BBC censorship did not spill over into other literary work was no accident. The terms of the BBC contract precluded doing any outside work of this kind without permission and this was seldom given. Indeed the copyright of work he did whilst with the BBC was the BBC's copyright, not Orwell's, a matter which caused considerable difficulty when the material was first published in 1985. There were well-known cases of BBC employees having written full-length books which the BBC then refused to allow to be published because they had been written whilst the person concerned was a BBC employee. Had *Animal Farm* been written whilst Orwell was at the BBC, for example, and if this could have been proved, the copyright would have been the BBC's.

It is clear from this that Orwell was being censored before 1944 as well, it simply was that the fact remained unknown and a purely internal affair at the BBC until the publication of his broadcasts and the archive material in 1985. When Orwell left the BBC he began writing as an independent person again and almost immediately fell foul of the authorities who were without doubt waiting to see what he was going to do when he was out on his own.

Second, Gleb Struve was not the only person to know that a politically 'difficult' book was to appear from Orwell's pen early in 1944. Eileen freely discussed the book with friends in the Ministry of Food, and no doubt Orwell dropped similar hints to his colleagues at *Tribune* and elsewhere. The result of this would have been to alert all censors. How they came across Orwell's text when they did is still a mystery. Orwell's letter to Gollancz first telling him of the book is dated 19 March 1944, three days after the sudden stopping of his review of Laski's book. However in his letter Orwell refers to the typing which would be completed in a few days. Since he also says that he had finished the book the clear implication is that he had got someone else to type it. Present day experience suggests that the authorities have no difficulty obtaining advance copies of typescripts when it is necessary; presumably they had similar systems in operation then. Or perhaps the very fact that he had actually written something which was going to publishers was enough. The proximity of the dates makes it clear that action was somehow precipitated at the time the *Animal Farm* text first appeared and then left in place. The result of the action the censors then set in train is highly important for *Nineteen Eighty-Four* for it started Orwell off on lines of thought which caused him greater and greater confusion, exaggerating his sense of isolation. The banning of his review of Laski's piece puzzled him. Writing to Dwight Macdonald, the editor of *Politics*, he said (Macdonald's direct quotation in an editorial in *Politics* for November 1944):

> I thought it might amuse you to see the review I wrote of it [Laski's book] when first published. This review was written for the *Manchester Guardian* (generally looked on as the most truthful paper in England). The Editor refused to print it, evidently because of its anti-Stalin implications. If you look through it you will see that I have gone as far as was consistent with ordinary honesty *not* to say what pernicious tripe the book is, and yet my remarks were too strong even for the *Manchester Evening News*. This will give you an idea of the kind of thing you can't print in England nowadays.

The double edge to this plea from Orwell, his saying that he had done as much as humanly possible not to transgress the political guidelines, was that it was written knowing that the letter would pass through the censorship in Liverpool and go onto his file. He seems at times to have been actually conducting a dialogue with the censors. This might appear to be so far-fetched as to suggest conspiracy theory, were it not for the fact that one censor did at last write to him suggesting that if he wanted detailed discussion of what they intended to take out and leave in, rather than a letter after the event, then he should put a telephone number on the back of the envelope as well as his address so that he could be phoned during the day! Clearly Orwell was an awkward customer, and they knew he was and decided to meet him half way. They could not have done this without authority, and the question of Orwell's relationships with the security services will be discussed in chapter fourteen. The day to day results of the censorship were not affected by this concession at the time that *Animal Farm* and the other texts were blocked.

Writing to Philip Rahv, editor of *Partisan Review*, Orwell showed signs of anxiety on the score of censorship, so much so that he wrote, in a letter which he knew would be seen by the censor:

> I sent off my London Letter on about April 17th, so that should certainly reach you before the end of May unless held up in the censorship. After I had sent it off it struck me that there were several things in it the censorship might object to (on policy grounds, not security of course), but I haven't had any note from them to say they were stopping it, so I suppose its all right. Your letter hadn't been opened by the censor by the way.

Any censor reading this would know Orwell was aware of the distinction between Policy and Security censorship and pass it to his superiors in view of its content. Orwell received no letter in return this time but if he was looking for any clue about *Animal Farm* he failed to get it, despite filling the second half of his letter to Rahv with an extensive and pointed account of the difficulty he was having in getting his book published. This is the clearest indication that Orwell suspected it was being banned by the MOI. However he does not himself seem to have gone on and made any connection between this and the various other occasions his work was being stopped. It may of course have been that he knew he would be wasting his time, unless, like Winston Smith, he kept a separate record. And this of course is exactly what *Nineteen Eighty-Four* became.

Before looking at the troubled publishing history of *Animal Farm* another of the banned texts, his essay on Salvador Dali, gives some interesting sidelights. For any publisher to go to the length of removing pages from bound copies of a book is an extreme measure. The cost is considerable and the logistics of finding a substitute piece and having it printed in a matter of hours, as happened in this case, was traumatic for the publisher's staff. Why was the essay suppressed? A note on the bottom of the pages substituted merely said the text had been removed for unavoidable reasons. These, also the ones given to Orwell, were that his review was obscene in its description of Dali's admittedly obscene book. A far more likely reason is to be found elsewhere in the text:

> Such people [leader writers of *The Times* etc.] are not only unable to admit that what is morally degrading can be aesthetically right, but their real demand of every artist is that he shall pat them on the back and tell them that thought is unnecessary. And they can be especially dangerous at a time like the present when the Ministry of Information and the British Council put power into their hands, for their impulse is not only to crush every new talent as it appears but to castrate the past as well.

The censors seem to have obliged by forcing the publishers either to pulp the book in its entirety or 'castrate' it as Orwell had effectively challenged them to do. The argument that obscenity was the actual reason falls because the book which Orwell was describing was not itself banned which would have been perfectly possible had the material fallen in that category, as Orwell would have known better than most after his first brush with the authorities over Henry Miller in those almost forgotten days before the war.

However much Orwell was annoyed by the censorship of his BBC talks he seems not to have believed that a work of pure fiction consciously modelled on his beloved Swift, a fairy story even as it was described on the title, could actually be banned. His first step had to be to submit *Animal Farm* to the publisher with whom he had a contract, Victor Gollancz. But he did not wish to have any delay and, knowing that Gollancz could not possibly publish it he first wrote asking him if he wanted to see it, as he had earlier rejected *Homage to Catalonia* sight unseen. Gollancz wrote back saying he could not understand why he should be denied the opportunity to see it, having forgotten his earlier behaviour. When he saw the force of Orwell's letter and that the book took an extreme anti-Stalin position which he could not back without doing his own firm serious damage, he capitulated. His reply was one of the shortest Gollancz letters on file:

> My Dear Blair [not Orwell]
> You were right and I was wrong. I am so sorry. I have returned the manuscript to Moore [Orwell's agent].
>
> > Yours sincerely,
> > Dictated by Mr. Gollancz
> > but signed in his absence.

The question, raised above, was whether Gollancz also kept a copy of the book and sent it to the MOI, or whether they had already got a copy. Gollancz would have alerted others to the book and its content, but that would not have been enough to arouse official interest of the kind which soon became obvious.

Orwell first offered the book to the young Andre Deutsch then working for Nicolson and Watson, a firm that was seen as very much of the left at the time, but which had unaccountable lapses, such as the appointment of Tambimuttu to run a poetry list, which may have encouraged Orwell to think he could get his book through. However the firm had not lost its way as much as that and he found himself arguing face-to-face with the chairman of the firm, J.A.C. Roberts, who told him exactly what he thought of his opinions on Russia. Deutsch, even then hankering after his own list, suggested that he publish it, but this proved impossible from a business point of view and so Orwell tried a third publisher, Cape. It was Cape who finally alerted him to what was happening, indirectly, by his actions. He was himself subject to MI5 scrutiny—see the intercepted letter illustrated here.

The book was read by Daniel George who gave it a conditional recommendation saying it would get many readers but adding the rider:

> Publication of it is a matter of policy. I cannot myself see any serious objection to it.

George was an experienced reader who also reviewed novels for *Tribune*. When he wrote that publication of it was 'a matter of policy' he was making a comment which Cape would have clearly understood, as we saw Orwell writing to his American editor that there may have been things to object to in his work on ground of 'policy'. But there was more still to George's comments, for he remarked that amongst those that would approve of the book were many who 'might not be of the class of which the author publicly approves'. He too, clearly, wished to distance himself from Orwell and may already have learnt that the text had attracted the attention of the MOI.

Cape stalled by querying the contract position with Gollancz whilst the manuscript was sent to the MOI. In a letter to Moore Cape says that he sent the book to 'a senior official' at the MOI without identifying him. The senior official responsible for this censorship was Francis Williams, and if he was not the actual person writing to Cape, such an important matter could not have gone through without his knowing. Further, as has been seen from the examples at the beginning of the chapter, there was almost certainly a general ban on Orwell when he was being even faintly contentious. These outright bans were few and far between and were a matter, indeed, for a 'senior official'.

Jonathan Cape's letter to Moore is a classic example of the kind of pressures censorship could bring to bear on a man who might in normal circumstances be the epitome of a liberal concerned publisher. The key passage referred is a simple repetition of the language used in the MOI cautions, so that Moore would understand its source:

> I can now see that it might be regarded as something which it was highly ill-advised to publish at the present time.

This pressure was not theoretical. The Emergency Powers regulations provided for the seizure of the presses of anyone publishing material that contravened the instructions of the MOI. No printer could possibly take such a risk, and since the publisher was the person who the printer depended on for his safety in such matters no printer would print for Cape again if he disobeyed such an instruction from the MOI. Orwell's biographer remarked that Orwell was torn between rage and tears and, indeed, it is almost incredible now that these draconian powers should have been exercised over such a book as *Animal Farm*.

After Cape's rejection Orwell tried to get T. S. Eliot to take the book for Faber and Faber, relying no doubt on the friendship he had built up during his BBC days, and the slight guilt Eliot must have felt for turning down Orwell's first book. Eliot's reply was a particularly tortured one. He explained that he had to rely on the verdict of at least one director besides himself, and then went on to try and show that no one in the firm really supported the thesis of the story anyway, as if they were involved in the same political crusade as Orwell and differed over tactics:

> Now I think my own dissatisfaction with this apologue is that the effect is simply one of negation. It ought to excite some sympathy with what the author wants, as well as sympathy with his objections to something; and the positive point of view, which I take to be generally Trotskyite, is not convincing.

In its way Eliot's intellectual posturing is simply another variety of doublethink. Orwell had already fired the warning shot in his letter to Eliot:

> Cape, or the MOI, I am not certain which from the wording of his letter, made the imbecile suggestion that some other animal than pigs might be made to represent the Bolsheviks. I could not of course make any change of that description.

A phone call would have told Eliot, or Geoffrey Faber, since it was he that was finally responsible, that the book could not be published. That Eliot fully understood this can be seen from one final parting shot which revealed a less than pleasant side of his character and showed the bureaucrat just below the surface (a publisher/author is still an unusual person):

> I am very sorry because whoever publishes this will naturally have the opportunity of publishing your future work: and I have a regard for your work, because it is good writing of fundamental integrity . . .

The message perhaps was that the book was banned and Orwell had better think of the consequences for his future work. The patronising reference to the 'fundamental integrity' of Orwell's work was emphasised a few lines earlier when he compared the book to Swift's *Gulliver*; the intellectual loophole Eliot seems to have left himself was that *Animal Farm* was *not* a work of integrity. Unless Geoffrey Faber did not spell things out for him, and he actually carried on as a wartime publisher

115

without knowing in any detail the regime he was operating under, then Eliot was simply being hypocritical. The reason he could not publish was that the MOI would not allow it to be published. And this message was reiterated, albeit in coded form, by the publisher who finally agreed to publish it, Fred Warburg.

Before going to the BBC Orwell had been editing the Searchlight series with Tosco Fyvel for Warburg. It has been said that the series ended when the back stock was lost in the blitz but there are reasons, to be mentioned shortly, for thinking this was not so. It is also known that Warburg turned down Orwell's part of the joint wartime diary he was writing with Inez Holden—and indeed Inez's diary was published by Bodley Head not Warburg. What happened to cause these events is not known but there must have been a parting of the ways of some kind which would make Orwell naturally reluctant to reapproach Warburg. Orwell's authorised biographer has suggested that he was the natural choice and that perhaps Orwell did not approach him at first because he wanted one of the top-line publishers for a book as important as he thought *Animal Farm* to be. Orwell did not think like that, although there was an element of truth here. Secker and Warburg were not then the major house they subsequently became, in particular they did not have the previous backlists and publishing schedules which guaranteed them in advance that they would have adequate stocks of that vital pre-requisite in publishing—paper.

When Orwell approached Warburg he had already been told that he might be interested. This proved to be the case but his agreeing to do the book depended on the vital aspect of paper. The MOI would have known about Warburg's paper situation, indeed they had direct control of the supply of paper to publishers under certain circumstances: on one occasion paper supply for export copies of an edition of *Horizon* was going to be withheld unless an article was altered. When *Animal Farm* finally did appear after the war had ended the dust-wrapper was printed on the reverse of jackets that had been pre-printed for books in the Searchlight Books series. Presumably the paper stock was still in such short supply that these had to be used, giving the lie incidentally to the suggestion that the paper stocks being lost in the blitz were the reason for the Searchlight series ending. Surviving copies of the first edition of *Animal Farm* are frequently found with the jackets printed on this stock.

Warburg's decision to sign up the book was a very shrewd one. He realised that things were changing and that Orwell's book, whilst anathema in 1944, might soon become acceptable and that he would indeed, as Eliot said, have the option on Orwell's future books. However his decision had to be made in such terms that he could give reasons when required for delays in publication as he knew that, in fact, he could *not* publish it without the MOI's agreement. This seems to have been concealed from Orwell and also his agent and may be one of the reasons that Orwell never fully understood what was happening. If Warburg was prepared to accept the book then the others must have had political or other reasons, lack of courage in Eliot's case no doubt, for not taking the book.

The slow rise of *Animal Farm* from the murky depths of wartime censorship had begun but the light was still some way above and it did not finally appear until not merely the war but the election that followed it was over. In the meantime Orwell found himself saddled with uncongenial journalism which, paradoxically, many have subsequently seen as his best work. There is of course no way of knowing what the effect of *Animal Farm* would have been if it had not been banned. It would have been politically controversial and might even have become a factor in the debate over how Germany was to be treated after the war—with special reference to the likely role Stalin's Russia was to play in Europe. The MOI files relating to the banning of *Animal Farm*, and other similar happenings, have not been found so it is not possible to know what the grounds given by Francis Williams were if Brendan Bracken or anyone else asked him for an explanation. The activities of the MOI were secret and the contingency plans in the event of future conflicts no doubt follow similar lines even now, so it is unlikely that any Freedom of Information Act would enable the material to be released, were the entire episode not so shaming that it is highly likely all the material has long ago been destroyed. If they still exist then the publication of them would enable us to see more clearly one of the major forces that led Orwell to create his next work, *Nineteen Eighty-Four*.

CHAPTER ELEVEN

Finding a Dream

There are moments of happiness in Julia and Winston's brief affair, ended in a few months by 'the Thought Police'. Apart from regular meetings in a rented room above a shop in a London back-street the most memorable are those spent out in the countryside. It is there that the affair starts and the countryside is part of it. Whether there was an 'original' of Julia in Orwell's own life or not, the country undoubtedly did provide the one solace and hope for Orwell and Eileen, and the countryside occurs in Orwell's work repeatedly. Even in wartime London he remarks on things such as the willowherb amongst the bombed sites, and a heron flying over the park, and Eileen felt exactly the same way. In her last letter to Orwell she said 'I don't think you understand what a nightmare the London life is to me'; and although Orwell kept up the essential cameraderie of the wartime pub life, he could write to his American audience:

> This has been a foul summer, everything happening at the wrong time and hardly any fruit. I have been tied so tight to this beastly town that for the first time in my life I have not heard a cuckoo this year.

The Orwell of the pub and his 'As I please' journalism was a completely different person capable of making fun of people who wrote to the papers claiming to have heard the first cuckoo of the year. The feeling behind his outburst against 'this beastly town' cannot be disguised. There were those who knew him in London who claimed that he fitted into the wartime London life of the Blitz and blackout as into an old sports jacket. Nothing could have been further from the truth. He was far closer to Eileen's view of that kind of life which eventually helped to kill her. She once confided to Tosco Fyvel, who noticed that she seemed unhappy in one of the Fitzrovia pubs that Orwell and his colleagues frequented, that she only drank bitter beer in the smallest glass because she did not actually like it. One of her pet aversions was eating out in public which was, she thought, a barbaric ritual, at least in London.

Although, as we saw in chapter two, Eileen was the first to go to London and plunge into 'war work', whilst Orwell clung to the rural idyll which had been the home they married into, she shared with Orwell an urgent desire to get away as soon as possible. From 1940 Orwell had begun to develop a dream that seems to have helped him right through the worst years of the war, a dream he in turn shared with Eileen, that of a home on one of the Hebridean islands described so rapturously by Compton Mackenzie. He wrote in his diary for 20 June 1940:

> Thinking always of my island in the Hebrides, which I suppose I shall never possess or even see. Compton Mackenzie says even now most of the islands are uninhabited (there are 500 of them, only 10% inhabited at normal times), and most have water and a little cultivable land and goats will live on them.

It is the detail of the goats which tells us that this was something more than a fantasy for Orwell; he had goats at Willington and had lived off goat's milk and cheese. Compton Mackenzie had been one of the first serious critics who had praised Orwell's work unreservedly from the beginning. It was support Orwell valued and he admired Mackenzie and believed what he said about the islands.

Orwell talked about the Hebrides, and the possibility of living there, with many wartime colleagues. Eileen would have been happy with a cottage anywhere in the country as long as it was away from London and most of his friends would have thought his idea of an island a little wild. But Orwell was from a family where places as far away as Burma were a second home, even, as we have suggested in the introduction, their real home. The Hebrides would seem almost next door by comparison. This perspective was the genuine colonial one and it would have been shared by people at Eton and from that background. A place in Scotland with shooting in the season was the upper-class equivalent of the southern middle-class cottage in the country. Nor would the idea appeal only to those interested in sport—since the days of the poet Clough there had always been the romantic image of a bothie somewhere far away, and if on an island so much the better.

In a first step towards a more bearable life the Orwells left their modernist flat in Victory Mansions for a more comfortable Victorian house in Maida Vale with a basement where Orwell could set up his lathe and woodwork shop. Shortly after his mother and sister came to live in a house nearby. The move must have been a great upheaval, particularly for his mother as she was not well and yet insisted on getting a job at Selfridges department store. This work is exhausting for someone of sound health used to the life. Ida Blair filled neither of these qualifications and, tragically, she collapsed at Selfridges and died in hospital a week later. The effect on Orwell can be imagined, despite comment made later by his authorised biographer that he never spoke about it. Winston's belief, in *Nineteen Eighty-Four*, that he had somehow caused the death of his mother points in an entirely different direction. Eileen would have been reminded of the death of her brother. To add to their misery the one reason they had gone to live in Victory Mansions was borne out in practice when their new flat was blitzed. It was not a direct hit—the manuscript of *Animal Farm* was retrieved from the wrecked building—but

121

their home had to be demolished. They went to stay in Inez Holden's flat and then at last found another flat in Islington. With every move they must have longed even more for their island home. From June 1944 there was an additional reason, for Eileen had left her job with the Ministry of Food and adopted a son, Richard Blair.

Sometime in 1944 Orwell heard that there was a deserted farmhouse for let at a nominal rent on Jura. It has been said that Orwell first heard of Jura through David Astor, and went to the island in 1945 for a brief stay with Astor, and then stayed a fortnight with an elderly couple at the north of the island who lived in a cottage on the Fletcher Estate, as it later became. However it is quite clear that there must have been some earlier introduction, for Eileen's first letters enquiring about the house were addressed not to Mrs Fletcher (née Brown) but to Sandy Brown her brother. He had been in London at the time but was killed on active service in 1944. Mrs Fletcher inherited the estate when her brother died and ran it until her husband Robin Fletcher came back from a Japanese concentration camp. She continued the correspondence with Eileen which was practical, concerned with questions such as food and how to survive in a place over twenty miles from the nearest shop. Eileen had lived in a cottage without electricity or hot water and with only primitive sanitation and knew the likely problems. Although the question of how the Orwells got to know about Barnhill is of interest, it might well be that no answer will ever be found. In the end it was David Astor who also had an estate on Jura whose interest was to prove the catalyst that made the project actually work when it seemed very unlikely that it would.

David Astor had been a good friend to Orwell since first meeting him during the war as proprietor of the *Observer* and had offered him the foreign correspondent's post for the paper in North Africa. This had been one of the factors that had boosted Orwell's courage when it came to actually leaving the BBC. This job had fallen through for the good reasons already examined. Now, with the imminent fall of Germany

122

in Europe, another job was found there which did not involve quite the health risks of North Africa. Orwell was finding life in London more and more difficult and the journalism an impossible distraction from the work he wanted to get on with, preferably away from it all on Jura. He leapt at the chance Astor gave him and this time there was no problem with the army medical boards which Orwell had to go through again, as war correspondents held military rank—Orwell was known as Captain Eric Blair.

Orwell has been severely criticised for going off to Europe in this way, particularly because Eileen was shortly to have an operation. The authorised biographer relates:

> He was too caught up in his fascination with the last days of the Third Reich to give proper attention to the situation at home, and he was accustomed to thinking Eileen could manage without him. He had his work to do and she had hers, and that was that. Neither would accomplish anything if they spent too much time worrying about the other.

These deeply offensive remarks have not one whit of evidence to back them up; the statement that he was accustomed to thinking that Eileen could get on without him is at odds with all the actual evidence of the reality of their marriage and the struggles they had gone through together. In fact the reasons for Orwell's going to Europe are plain for anyone to see. Both Orwell and Eileen were intent on leaving London: her last letter to him makes this abundantly clear and she had been making the actual arrangements to go to Jura. The problem with these plans was that they had no money with which to make the move. Taking their furniture to Jura would be an expensive job and the legal and other problems in winding down their various other properties—they had sub-let their previous flats off Baker Street and in Islington—and removing things from them to store would also be costly. When they had made lengthy journeys before, such as that to North Africa before the war, money had come as a loan of £300 which was subsequently repaid. Now there was a need for a further sum which would have to have added to it some part of the income he would lose through his loss of the journalism, however despised.

Seen in this light David Astor's offer—an opportunity to acquire a large lump sum—must have come as a godsend. Indeed since he was close to their future home in Jura it might be thought he made the offer with that in mind, wrongly, for he was unaware that Orwell was actually going to live on Jura at this time. His account shows clearly that he was unaware that Eileen and George had set their heart on a life at Barnhill in 1944. It is now known that Eileen realised that she would have to have an operation of some kind even before she adopted their son. Orwell's going off to Europe offered her the ideal opportunity to have this done whilst he was away. There was a serious miscalculation in this plan, however, which in peacetime would have made no difference; in her much-reduced state of health it did have disastrous results.

Those who have said that Orwell was acting with callous indifference when he went off to Europe have ignored or not understood important pointers to the contrary. Orwell knew very well that his health was extremely bad. He specifically mentioned that he had been refused the North Africa post because he might not survive and then Eileen would have got a pension for the rest of her life. The same thing applied when he went to Europe. As he might have expected the rigours of the journey produced a relapse and a haemorrhage whilst he was in Cologne. Far from showing lack of care for Eileen and Richard—to whom he was totally attached—he drew up some notes to guide his literary executor which he sent off to Eileen to be witnessed. It is quite clear that he thought he was going to die in Cologne as there can be no other explanation for drawing up such a document which he had not done before despite his other serious bouts of illness. Far from his going to Europe showing lack of care for his family it showed compassion and love taken to the point where he was prepared to die, literally, knowing that either he would raise enough for them all to go and live

124

on Jura or he would actually die, in which case they would be provided for.

There seems to be little excuse for those who have written in disparaging terms about Orwell going to Europe. This is particularly the case because the great risk he took was set at nothing by the completely unexpected tragedy of Eileen's death. The miscalculation mentioned earlier was over the question of time needed for her to build up strength before undergoing an operation. The hospital in London, aware of the strain that people living through the Blitz on low food intake had suffered, warned that some period in hospital before the operation could be carried out was essential. Eileen thought their concerns exaggerated and went instead to a hospital in the north of England, near where her sister-in-law lived. They could see no danger and she went ahead with the operation. However her weakness and exhaustion were real. Almost immediately after the anaesthetic was applied she collapsed and died. The death certificate mentioned specifically that the anaesthetic had been properly administered. Nor could any blame be laid at the door of doctors who could not be expected to understand the real changes that five years of deprivation had wrought on the constitutions of Londoners. Eileen had not expected the operation to be very serious. She wrote a letter which she meant to finish after she came round and, perhaps even more poignantly, the day following her death Orwell's letter containing his proposed will and literary executor's instructions arrived for her signature.

Orwell heard of her death in hospital in Cologne, discharged himself with a strong dose of M&B tablets and flew back to England. He went straight to Inez Holden's flat, to which she had now returned, and his appearance was so changed that she scarcely recognised him. Her account in her unpublished diary shows that he was profoundly upset and still very ill. Despite this he immediately went north and arranged the funeral himself.

If anyone's life can be said to have fallen apart, Orwell's

had at this moment. His immediate worry was clearly Richard. Having arranged for him to be looked after by his sister-in-law for a few months he decided, astonishingly, to carry on with their plan to move to Jura. Perhaps Eileen's last letter encouraged him to do this. She urged him to drop reviewing and get away from the 'literary life'. Jura was still there and he could continue the arrangements; but for that to go ahead he still needed to carry on with his *Observer* work and he clearly decided that was what Eileen would have wanted him to do. Eileen had died on 29 March, 1945. By about 8 April he was in Paris again, travelling to Germany before returning to Paris for VE-Day, then going to Austria before coming back to London near the end of May.

The experience of being in Paris on VE-Day must have been exhilarating especially as he was there as a war correspondent for one of the most prestigious London papers, when all those years before he had been a *plongeur* (a dishwasher) at a restaurant and as down as it was possible to be. Had he lived longer no doubt he would have incorporated some of what he saw and felt in a novel. Instead he returned to a wartorn London that was essentially unchanged, with the same political back-biting and squabbling he had left behind. The temptation to have Richard adopted again would have been great but the idea never appears to have entered Orwell's mind.

Despite Warburg's assurances *Animal Farm* had still not been published when the general election campaign of June and July 1945 began. Orwell covered the campaign for The *Observer*, but must have been the only journalist who had a best-selling book which was being held back because of the election and the effect it might have on it. Orwell makes this quite plain in a letter he wrote to his friend Herbert Read the day after *Animal Farm* finally appeared, 17 August, 1945:

I am probably going to continue my column [in *Tribune*] or something similar, after I come back from my holiday. I stopped it, of course, while I was in France and didn't start again because Bevan was terrified there might be a row about *Animal Farm*, which might have been embarrassing if the book had come out before the election, as it was first intended to.

The rule of the MOI and the D-notice still ran, despite the ending of the war in Europe. Bevan's consciousness of the book which was, after all, only a fairy story is no doubt linked with the extraordinary events that took place within the Labour Party immediately after the election. Francis Williams describes the abortive putsch that attempted to remove Attlee and the part played in it by such figures as Maurice Webb. This is not, perhaps, the best place to look at the political in-fighting that went on at this time and Bevan's role. Orwell knew simply that his book was postponed yet again. When it did finally appear it was an instant success, and the American edition even more so.

The genuineness of his feelings for Eileen and his determination to carry on with the dream of his home in the Hebrides can be seen in a letter he wrote to Max Plowman's widow, regretting that Eileen had not been alive to see *Animal Farm*'s great success. The holiday he referred to in his letter to Herbert Read was on Jura and he called on the Fletchers and continued with the negotiations which Eileen had begun. However strong his desire to stay, without Eileen it was going to take a lot more effort to set up a home in such a remote spot. Orwell would have realised, perhaps for the first time, exactly what lay behind Eileen's practical questions. Also he wanted to raise his son there, and without a wife that could prove difficult. Most of his friends who knew of his interest in Jura thought he would give up the idea, just as they thought it likely that he would have Richard re-adopted.

Inez Holden who later visited Jura, and was certainly close to Orwell and Eileen, watched over Orwell from the moment he appeared on her doorstep back from Germany. After he came back from Jura, so unsure was he of his final purpose, that he seriously considered going to a farm in the country with Inez.

The letters disclosing this in the Orwell archive do not make clear what kind of life they would be leading, or, if Richard was there, whether she would be involved in bringing him up. Unfortunately Inez's diaries are closed so the facts cannot be determined for certain. What is clear is that the proposal, which was serious enough to involve discussion of the rent being asked, came to nothing, and when Inez came to Jura on a visit later she did not stay for very long.

Orwell clearly needed time to arrange things and so he returned from his holiday (as he had told Read he would) and plunged back into London literary life, resuming his old column and his articles. He lived in the flat in Islington with Richard, Eileen's place being filled as far as he was concerned by the very middle-class solution of a nurse who came by recommendation, Susan Watson. The experiment was not a success in the long run although she managed well enough in London, and Orwell cannot have been an easy person to life with for anyone not used to the incessant pounding of a typewriter. He must also have been lonely, and the fact that most of what he was typing was journalism of a kind that he despised and that he knew Eileen had warned him specifically against cannot have helped. In a letter to his agent Moore, written as early as June 1945, he said he was starting work on a new novel, which was *Nineteen Eighty-Four*, but he seems to have done nothing except develop themes that appeared in the book as he had done before the war ended. They form a continuous development which was also closely linked to the political situation he found himself in and which helped contribute to Orwell's growing isolation.

CHAPTER TWELVE

The Political Struggle 1944–45

Although Orwell was well known for being able to see both sides of a question, to the point of making favourable comment about Hilter, as we have seen, one person it would be almost impossible to imagine him giving a point to was Stalin. Yet even that could happen, if only in a private letter to someone he thought he knew well. The impossible happened in a letter written from Paris to Roger Senhouse in March 1945. *Animal Farm* was at the final stages before it was due to go to press and Orwell wrote to Senhouse with a last minute alteration to be inserted 'If it has not actually been printed yet'. He wrote saying that whereas he had originally described the pig Napoleon flinging himself on his face when the windmill was blown up, he now thought it only right that this should be changed to 'all the animals except Napoleon'. The explanation was his earnest desire to be even-handed, even with such a butcher as Stalin:

If the book has been printed it's not worth bothering about but I just thought the alteration would be fair to J[oseph] S[talin], as he did stay in Moscow during the German advance.

There is a distinct possibility that this suggestion was made as a deliberate dig at Senhouse. The letter had begun by thanking him for sending Orwell a copy of *Homage to Catalonia* as he had given his own copy to someone he first thought

129

was Andre Malraux but in fact turned out to be Jose Rovira, the commander of Orwell's division in Spain who Orwell said he had just met in a friend's house. Little is known of Senhouse's political views, or of his own career other than that he was a bibliophile. In fact he was an intimate friend of Guy Burgess and frequently went on holidays with him. The slightly cynical tone in the dust jacket blurb for *Animal Farm*, and later for *Nineteen Eighty-Four*, suggests that he was not wholly sympathetic to Orwell's views. Had he been retailing the goings on at what was often called the Trotskyist publishing house to Burgess, then he would have relished being able to identify Orwell as still being in the circle around Rovira. In mentioning this, and then immediately after suggesting a miniscule alteration to be fair to Stalin, Orwell appears to have realised that it was worth pulling Senhouse's leg over such things.

Even now the revelation that Orwell was meeting Rovira is tantalising and makes it all the more annoying that he left no more detailed record of his life in Paris. His meeting with Ernest Hemingway has been described often and an entire novel was written starting out from the suggestion that Orwell borrowed a service revolver from Hemingway because he thought someone was out to kill him, someone whom he had first met in Spain. That he was able to see his time in Spain and the aftermath of the war in Europe in a single perspective was remarkable. Most people who had been involved in Spain had had their loyalties turned and turned about as first the Nazi-Soviet pact, then the Nazi invasion of Russia tore their loyalties one way then another. In an article in 1944 Orwell had written:

There is violent competition by all parties to cash in on the popularity of the USSR. The pinks deprecate any criticism of the USSR on the ground that it 'plays into the hands of the Tories', but on the other hand the Tories seem to be the most pro-Russian of the lot. From the point of view of the MOI and the BBC, the only two people who are completely sacrosanct are Stalin and Franco.

The illogicality of seeing Franco and Stalin as equally sacrosanct puzzled Orwell and became a central element in *Nineteen Eighty-Four*, for he saw that the explanation was the linking of a kind of leader-worship with an almost schizophrenic view of life which enabled people to hold two contradictory points of view in their head at the same time and believe both. In his book he enunciates this as one of the principles of Newspeak; he arrived at the idea over a period of eighteen months or more, variations of it surfacing in his articles throughout that period. He referred again to the need not to offend Franco in an essay 'Through a Glass Rosily'. In that case it was Catholic papers in 1941 who suggested that criticising Franco would drive him into the arms of the axis, the exact logic behind the MOI and BBC edicts that Franco was not to be criticised in the media. He compared that with the situation when he was writing in November 1945 when he was being told on all sides not to criticise Russia, no matter what she did, as this was playing into the fascists' hands and he compared this again with his own most recent experience at the hands of the censors:

> I have had writings of my own kept out of print because it was feared the Russians would not like them, and I have had others kept out of print because they attacked British imperialism and might be quoted by anti- British Americans. We are told *now* that any frank criticism of the Stalin regime will 'increase Russian suspicions' but it is only seven years since we were being told (in some cases by the same newspapers) that frank criticism of the Nazi regime would increase Hitler's suspicions.

There were endless variations on this theme which have a faint modern echo in the suggestion that people vote 'tactically' in an election, which means in fact voting for something or someone they don't believe in because if they do not they will be 'playing into the hands' of the Tories or whoever it is thought necessary to get rid of. In the same article he referred to the use the German broadcasters had made of works of E.M. Forster such as *A Passage to India* without even, as he said, having to resort to dishonest quotation. He even alluded directly to the use the Germans made of his own books.

But primarily the problem, he realised, was tied up with a combination of leader-worship and nationalism, although he gave his own meaning to the word nationalism. The concept had been extended in the twentieth century owing to the decrease of distances and the arrival of international media and the rapid, even instant international spread of ideas. In Orwell's terms they included communism, Zionism, anti-Semitism, Trotskyism and pacifism, usually associated with some power block or group. He very shrewdly pointed out that there had often in the past, amongst British intellectuals, been a transference of their national loyalties to another country. Lafcadio Hearne became absorbed by Japan—an interest which was shared by many before the First World War when Japan was Britain's ally. In the middle of the nineteenth century there was great interest in Germany, partly through the influence of people such as Carlyle and partly through the links between the British and German royal families. In Orwell's own day the British intelligentsia was irresistibly drawn to Russia. Although Orwell did not know about the treachery of people such as Burgess, or that even his own editor was so close to him, he realised that this split loyalty had entered the national consciousness in a profound way.

It was thinking along these lines that created many of the basic ideas in *Nineteen Eighty-Four*. Reading parts of his essay on nationalism it is often difficult to stop oneself thinking the text is not taken from, say, Goldstein's book in *Nineteen Eighty-Four* itself:

Every nationalist is haunted by the belief that the past can be altered. He spends part of his time in a fantasy world in which things happen as they should . . . and he will transfer fragments of this world to the history books whenever possible. Much of the propagandist writing of our time amounts to plain forgery. Material facts are suppressed, dates altered, quotations removed from their context and doctored so as to change their meaning. Events which, it is felt, ought not to have happened are left unmentioned and ultimately denied.

This was written in May 1945. By March the following year he had developed the idea still further. Writing in an essay called 'In front of your nose' he commented on the fact that people were explaining the coal shortage by saying it was impossible to get people to go down the pits and yet the same people were objecting to Polish and German miners being brought into the country because it would cause unemployment. In a crucial passage he showed he had succeeded in concentrating his complex thoughts on people's political allegiance to powers that were actually totalitarian. He chose a simple example like the coalmine question rather than the more contentious problems such as people who condemned the Nazi concentration camps and gas ovens and yet would not condemn, refused even to believe, that atrocities had occurred in Russia:

Medically, I believe, this manner of thinking is called schizophrenia: at any rate it is the power of holding simultaneously two beliefs which cancel out. Closely allied to it is the power of ignoring facts which are obvious and unalterable and which will have to be faced sooner or later. It is especially in our political thinking that these vices flourish.

It was the 'political thinking' of those around him that led him to write these articles which were extensive and

133

complex and, for him, an inescapable part of the London life he despised.

The failure of the postwar Labour government to do anything to alleviate the wartime shortages—they actually became worse—led to extensive activity on the left, largely Communist Party inspired. Orwell was seen as an enemy of the most extreme kind. He was not without allies and joined an organisation which stepped in to help people in conflict with authority when it was realised that the Civil Liberties Union had become a communist-front organisation. Other members were Herbert Read, Bertrand Russell, E.M. Forster and Hugh Slater, editor of *Polemic* which published some of the best of Orwell's work, including the essay referred to here 'Notes on Nationalism'. But however sympathetic they were the actual confrontation fell to Orwell, particularly as he was the author of the most savage attack against Stalin anyone had dared to make in *Animal Farm*.

We have already mentioned the close connection between *Animal Farm* and *Nineteen Eighty-Four* shown by Orwell's referring to both as having been created by the conference in Tehran, when the world was allocated into different spheres of interest. In his articles and essays he explored this theme over the months as he developed in parallel the theme of nationalism and the schizophrenic thought processes of those who believed in the godlike leaders of such groups. He wrote in his 'As I please' column for 2 February, 1945:

The way the world is actually shaping it may well be that war will *become permanent*. Already, quite visibly and more or less with the acquiescence of all of us, the world is splitting up into two or three super-states . . . If these two or three superstates do establish themselves not only will each of them be too big to be conquered, but they will be under no necessity to trade with each other and in a position to prevent all contact with other nationals. Already for a dozen years or so, large areas of the earth have been cut off from one another, although technically at peace.

By the autumn of 1945 he had developed and expanded this idea in his London letter to *Partisan Review*. He looked particularly at the future relationship between Britain and America which might possibly develop if the growth of the power blocs continued. This is precisely the analysis that is the basis of *Nineteen Eighty-Four* and is in fact a very accurate forecast of problems which still face Britain today. He examined the three possible arrangements of power blocs after the war, assuming that Britain was not strong enough to compete in the superpower league. The first was to struggle on. The second was to link up on a permanent basis with America—this was the situation in *Nineteen Eighty-Four*—or finally, to sever connection with India and the old Commonwealth and form what he called 'a solid bloc with the western European States and their African possessions'. This is in effect the European Community, although few analysts today would be able to link the decision to give India independence with the possibility of going into Europe. Again in *Nineteen Eighty-Four* there is continual change between these arrangements and the fighting that goes on in Africa is understandable. Today, with the African colonies liberated, the roots of the idea in his book have become obscured.

If his development of this idea is relatively clear and lucid in comparison with the earlier ideas on nationality and schizophrenia, there was another group of ideas which showed even greater signs of the strain Orwell was under at the time, verging on a breakdown in his own sanity perhaps, which is reflected directly at the heart of *Nineteen Eighty-Four*. The idea first occurs in a letter written to a private person H. J. Willmett who had simply written in to him as an author asking about totalitarianism and leader worship. Orwell first made a lucid statement of his ideas on nationalism and the disappearance of objective truth because what the leader said at any one time had to be the truth, and that 'already history in a sense had ceased to exist'. He went on to talk about Hitler who was in fact as much a model for 'Big Brother' as Stalin:

> Hitler can say the Jews started the war, and if he survives that will become official history. He can't say that two and two make five, because for the purpose of, say, ballistics, they have to make four. But if the sort of world that I am afraid of arrives, a world of two or three great superstates which are unable to conquer one another two and two could become five if the fuehrer [sic] wished it.

The remarkable thing about this letter, written absolutely candidly to someone who had simply written to him, is that Orwell himself seems to have come at this early stage to a clear understanding of the ideas that he was later to struggle over. Perhaps this is not surprising in the chaos of the time. The example which he stuck to through thick and thin, and which begins certainly to look like the clinging to an idea of a person close to breakdown, just as Winston was to do in *Nineteen Eighty-Four*, is the idea of two and two equalling five if the leader wished it. He repeats this idea with the same example the following year:

> So long as physical reality cannot be altogether ignored so long as two and two have to make four when you are, for example, drawing the blue-print of an aeroplane, the scientist has his function and can even be allowed his measure of liberty. His awakening will come later when the totalitarian state is firmly established. Meanwhile if he wants to safeguard the integrity of science it is his job to develop some kind of solidarity with his literary colleagues and not regard it as a matter of indifference when writers are silenced or driven to suicide, and newspapers systematically falsified.

It sounds as though there is some specific experience of

136

Orwell's here and there was. His interest in science, though that of an amateur, was genuine and went back to the days of H. G. Wells and his pioneering interest and popularisation of science through his text books as well as his tales of the future, his early science fiction. Orwell carried this through to a serious level when he established his science programmes at the BBC, such as 'A.D. 2000'. But the message here tells of *betrayal* by scientists. This plea for scientists to show solidarity with their writer colleagues, linked with the need to stick to such simple ideas as two plus two equals four, appears almost exactly replicated in *Nineteen Eighty-Four*. Winston is subjected to a modern form of torture, with white-coated scientists in the background operating the electrical machine, with the object not of getting him to reveal secrets, but to admit that two and two might make five! Who were these scientists that would happily go along with something like this? They would also fall within Orwell's schizophrenic category, since they would know more than anyone else that two and two did not make five, and yet would engage in torture to force someone to admit that it did. There were such people, in Orwell's eyes.

Andrew Gow, writing in his circular letters to his students and friends from Cambridge during the war, remarked that he did not know why scientists should be so closely connected with the Communist Party but they were. It is not known if Orwell was amongst those who got these letters—in view of the comments noticed in the introduction it is unlikely—but the scientists concerned were of a like mind to those who bothered Orwell, notably J.D. Bernal. Bernal was at Birkbeck when Orwell became involved in his political world, without fully understanding what he had come into contact with. After the war he made an extended attack on Bernal in an unsigned editorial in *Polemic*. Orwell's position was entirely consistent despite his not having the understanding which an opening of the records and the flight of Burgess has made clear to us.

We have mentioned how Bernal caused Orwell much

difficulty by first agreeing to host a series of scientific talks and then at the last minute withdrawing without explaining why. Orwell had subsequently called the series 'Science and Politics' which clearly implies that he understood that some political question had intervened; had he been in regular contact with Gow, with his knowledge of Cambridge communists, then he could perhaps have explained it to him. The link between scientists and the Communist Party was in full operation for Burgess, apparently alerted to Orwell's intended use of Bernal, wrote to him separately asking if he would like to do a series for the Home Service. This was the reason for the cancellation, and no doubt Burgess explained to Bernal exactly what was happening. There the matter ended at the time, one of the more unpleasant of Orwell's experiences at the BBC. Then, three years later in the December issue of *Modern Quarterly*, there appeared an attack on *Polemic* and an article by Bernal, both of which angered Orwell far more even than Humphrey Slater it seems, since Orwell who rarely did editorials for the magazine produced the answering essay in an anonymous editorial.

Orwell begins by quoting from an article by Bernal:

A radical change in morality is in any case required by the new social relations which men are already entering into in an organised and planned society. The relative importance of different virtues are bound to be affected. Old virtues may even appear as vices and new virtues instituted [*sic*]. Many of the basic virtues—truthfulness and good fellowship—are of course as old as humanity and need no changing but those based *on excessive concern with individual rectitude need reorienting in the direction of social responsibility*. [Orwell's emphasis]

He goes on to point out that this is tantamount to saying that 'we must alter our conception of right and wrong from year to year and if necessary from minute to minute'.

Here again is the rapid change of allegiance required of

party members that we have seen Orwell talk of before. He gives some of the familiar examples with new ones thrown in: in 1939 Soviet radio denounced the blockade of Germany as an attempt to starve the children there; in 1945 the starving of children in Germany and the shifting of masses of the population in their millions in Germany was considered a very good thing. Orwell pointedly remarked that presumably Bernal agreed with both statements. His choice of an example concerning children was not chance, of course, as he now had a small child of his own to look after in a London where rationing was in full operation. Bernal was a scientist, and yet he was quite capable of agreeing to fundamental shifts in human moral values simply because they had been deemed necessary by Russia. The worst example of the new moral values is one, again, which features specifically in *Nineteen Eighty-Four*, that of the praising of children who betrayed their parents. Readers of the book today will in the main have forgotten that such things happened, but they did, and on a systematic basis.

Pavlik Morozov was an 'official hero' in the Soviet Union for generations of young party members in the making. He died at the age of fourteen in 1932, murdered by relatives of his after denouncing his father and mother to the NKVD (the precursor of the KGB). His action was seen as a model by Stalin and the party and had become legendary even in Britain, where Bernal would have been the first to praise such heroic conduct as an example of the new virtues. In Russia today there has now been a reassessment in words which could have been taken from Orwell's mouth, but which were actually spoken by the novelist and historian Vladimir Amlinsky:

Pavlik Morozov, the hero, the image of a Pioneer-agent on which several generations were raised, is not a symbol of revolution and class consciousness but a symbol of legalised and romanticised treachery. [Under Stalin] there was no

139

good or evil. There was just class good and class evil, and they could be switched around at will.

In *Nineteen Eighty-Four* Orwell says this clearly. In postwar London, in 1946, he was having to argue such fundamental questions in the pages of magazines the majority of which would automatically have assumed Orwell to be in the wrong. Indeed (right up to the present day) some publications offering the orthodox opinions of the left in Britain have held Orwell in disdain for expressing such views. The peculiarly personal tone of the battle Orwell was fighting at the time stemmed from the closeness of London society and the almost universal sway that the Communist Party had come to hold through their secret members. The scientists such as Bernal were in the forefront of the campaign, certain a revolution would occur quite soon; but more damaging still were the remarks from people close to hand who were not just supposed friends but people who could affect the presentation of his actual work, such as Roger Senhouse. Even on *Tribune*, which he had to some extent made his home, with his idiosyncratic column, 'As I please', he was often told he was an unwelcome guest.

This kind of conflict would sap the creative will of any author, but when Orwell finally decided to leave it was for a more private reason. In letters to friends he explained that he wanted to get away from London so that his son might grow up away from life in a city. He wanted him to learn to walk in the countryside and not in the concrete wilderness of a city blitzed by war. It would also be a place where a child could learn that two plus two equalled four, and would go on doing so for the whole of his life and without developing a near paranoid fear that one day someone would torture him to try and make him believe that after all they made five.

Following this evolution of ideas, from leader-worship and schizophrenia through nationalism and the evolution of the superpowers, to the role of scientist and the folly of thinking two and two did not equal five if the leader said they did is complex enough now, even through brief extracts from key texts. For Orwell evolving these ideas in the face of continuing and bitter controversy of the most personal kind must have been an intolerable strain. Having grown used to working on his books with Eileen he must have missed her at such times and found that an added burden. But Richard was there, as a lasting symbol of their life together, and he pointed the way forward. His life was not to be lived in this kind of bickering, bomb-scarred wilderness. Jura beckoned.

141

CHAPTER THIRTEEN

Life on Jura

Writing in his novel *The Wind and the Waterfall*, set on a fictionalised Jura, Robert Gathorne-Hardy began: 'We have come to an island paradise.' He wrote in 1938 but a paradise it still was when Orwell finally set up home there, a refugee from the half-starved capital. The climate is mild because of the gulf-stream and it is often warmer than London though a little damper. Certainly Orwell would have been better off there than in the appallingly cold winters of 1946 and 1947 in London, when supplies became so bad and the cold so severe that he could write that he doubted if there would ever be a proper supply of coal again, and was reduced to burning furniture and even Richard's toys. On Jura there was peat in abundance and oil for the lamps and stoves came in forty-gallon drums; in London, he said, you had literally to go down on your knees to get half a gallon a week.

It is a pity that Orwell's hatred of London did not drive him straight up to Jura in the autumn of 1945 immediately after his first visit. He stayed on, spending Christmas with Arthur Koestler and his wife and sister-in-law in Wales but still returning to London once more. Then finally another domestic tragedy sent him off on the road north. His elder sister Marjorie Dakin died at the age of forty-eight and he attended her funeral at Nottingham, then, after a brief return to make final arrangements he went up to Biggar, near Edinburgh, and stayed briefly with a Spanish civil war friend

143

of his, George Kopp, now married to Doreen O'Shaugnessy half-sister to Eileen's sister-in-law, who had found Richard for them. The Kopps had also found the Orwells their home in Islington and had looked after Richard before Orwell obtained the nurse, Susan Watson.

The journey from Edinburgh to Jura took almost as long as it did to get from London to Edinburgh, and if there was any delay in coach or ferry times it could take days. There was a plane to the neighbouring island of Islay which Orwell used when the publication of *Animal Farm* transformed his financial situation, but at first he used the ferry which was then more direct than it is now, coming into Craighouse which has the island's only shop and hotel. From Craighouse Ardlussa, the Fletchers' estate, was twenty and more miles, and then seven miles beyond that was Barnhill which Orwell reached on 23 May, 1946. He stayed there alone for a week, entirely isolated, with the nearest telephone at Craighouse. Then he was joined by his sister Avril who helped him set the house in order before he went off down south again to fetch Richard and his nurse. The week he spent alone must have finally decided him that the venture was possible. His only neighbours were over a mile to the north at Kenuachdrach, running a small croft and fishing. He could see they were surviving and started to get the measure of the rhythm of life there, so different from that of London. Above all he could clear his mind of the day-to-day political and literary intrigue and gossip and begin to write again. If the roots of *Nineteen Eighty-Four* were originally in that London world, Jura made possible its growth; he transplanted his creation so thoroughly that even when he returned to London he left the drafts behind. The book was written on Jura and without the dream he had found with Eileen in 1944 it would *never* have been written.

For the first three months on Jura Orwell did almost no writing. The standard of living on the island, measured by such things as motor-cars, roads and telephones was low but in terms of food and climate things were immeasurably superior to life in London. He dropped occasional hints in letters to friends but, with rationing still in full force, he did not give too much away. Besides the deer, there were plentiful supplies of fish from lakes that were so remote they were hardly fished at all, and a daily routine was the journey out in the boat to check the lobster pots. Milk was brought from the croft, and flour and other necessities came up once a week from Ardlussa to the house, with the mail, sometimes brought more frequently if an estate worker was passing. When a television crew came to film Jura in 1983 in preparation for the worldwide mania about Orwell expected in the year 1984 itself, they found they had come to a place where there had been no change. Apart from some slight internal alterations and the installation of a (now) very elderly generator things were exactly as Orwell left them when he walked from the house for the last time with his great book finished. Around the house on every side was the other secret that Orwell kept from people in London—the stunning views and the island itself which Gathorne-Hardy rightly described as a paradise. Critics have agreed until now that the original of the 'golden country' in *Nineteen Eighty-Four* was the countryside near his cottage in Hertfordshire, but this probably reflects no more than that they could imagine life near Wallington but not that on Jura. There was a 'golden country' and one in which his son Richard actually did learn to walk and to look at the world as he and Eileen had hoped he would.

Orwell's presence on the island was unusual, but he fitted in roughly with the kind of people who occasionally came to shoot or tour the island. Gathorne-Hardy's book describes just such a world. Orwell himself was acting very much in keeping with his own background. Had he stayed in Burma for many years he would have returned to Britain, much as his father did, and settled in some place like Barnhill, although not perhaps one so remote. He had Compton Mackenzie to thank for that idea. It had been the normal thing for well over a century for people coming back from a tour of duty abroad to take a house somewhere. Orwell's move harked back to the sort of things done by the great nabobs as he called them. Barnhill, white on the hillside looking out across the sound of Jura, is not unlike Lambert Blair's house looked at from across the Exe estuary. There is strong evidence that Orwell could see that side of his life in his choosing to drop completely the name George Orwell when he came to Jura. He was always known there as Eric Blair, or Mr Blair and his family were called the Blairs, a widower living with an unmarried sister who was looking after his son. There were stranger households on Jura.

At the beginning Orwell kept on Susan Watson, Richard's nurse, but the situation was awkward. She had a physical impediment which affected her walking, and, as anyone who goes to Barnhill now would realise, this was an extremely serious handicap. There was a purely domestic problem also, for Orwell was paying her a substantial sum with all found, more than the best estate worker on Jura could hope to earn, for tasks which could be performed willingly by Orwell's sister, and often had to be anyway. Matters came to a head when a regular flow of visitors began arriving at Barnhill amongst whom was a boyfriend of Susan Watson, a young author who of course wished to live there also. This kind of ménage might be acceptable now, although some arrangement would have to be made about the costs involved; in Jura then it was unthinkable. There was no cottage available for them, and even had there been there was no work and they were not married. The arrangement ended rapidly, but sadly, with critics taking one side or another right up to the making of the film when these events were recreated nearly forty years later.

As Orwell slowly gathered his strength, doing some typing upstairs when ideas came to him, the stream of visitors grew. They were of two kinds: those to whom the journey was something completely out of the ordinary, an adventure, and others who had seen the world and came much in the same spirit as Orwell. He delighted in giving instructions for the journey from London which he knew would divide the sheep from the goats. Most of the bar-flies who were attracted by the romantic idea of living on a remote island were stopped by the first whiff of reality and never set out. Mostly Orwell was relieved, but there were exceptions: Sonia Brownell, eventually to marry Orwell on his death-bed, declined the journey and when she finally did come after his death did not conceal her distaste for the primitive living conditions she found there. Judging from his letter asking her to visit he must have been disappointed. However, others arrived including Inez, whose visit was perhaps the most serious of those who might have stayed longer.

The relationship between Orwell and Inez is puzzling. They had been considering setting up a household near London, as we have mentioned and her stay in Jura must have seemed to them both to be a real carrying-out of that intention. She had been very close to Eileen, and her cousin Celia Goodman was one of those to whom Orwell had proposed marriage after Eileen's death. During her stay she fitted in to the point of sitting at her typewriter in the kitchen and writing articles and stories which she would give to the mystified estate workers who called for the post, telling them the letters contained her manuscript and should go off with great urgency. In later life she recalled her visit to Jura in strangely domestic terms, for example criticising Orwell for suggesting that they could make passable matches, should the supply run out, by using sulphur. She saw this as evidence of his having a 'fantastically silly Robinson Crusoe' type of mind. It was more likely he was trying to explain that things were different in the winter on Jura when the ferry sometimes did not run for weeks and basic supplies could run out. The comments about Inez on Jura that have come down to us include Avril's remarks about her bringing a cat and various non-essential things, and inventing childish games such as one when she shouted out 'cannibals' whenever any strangers appeared, as they often did in the summer looking for milk or fuel for camp stoves, or a place to sleep. The echo of this game, with her own comment about Orwell's Robinson Crusoe approach to the world, rings true and suggests that there was some deep misunderstanding here, and an opportunity missed.

The other writers who appeared on Jura were all good friends of Inez and Orwell's, particularly Mulk Raj Anand and Paul Potts, although few got very close to him. Anand shortly went back to India and appears to have written nothing about the group at Barnhill. Paul Potts, who was a devoted admirer of Orwell's, has left a memorable portrait of life there in his *Dante Called You Beatrice*. He describes the arrival of Orwell's furniture:

> One day up on the Isle of Jura in the Hebrides we had to move some furniture from the nearest village to his house. . . . Some very rich people, friends of Orwell's, who had a hunting lodge on the other side of the island, had a whole garage full of brakes and wagons and jeeps—five I believe. Yet he refused to borrow the use of one for a few hours. We had to pack those chairs and that table on our backs across seven miles of some of the most beautiful scenery in Europe. This by a man who was a chronic invalid.

He did not notice the surreal element of seeing furniture which he had previously sat on in a comfortable flat in London suddenly being transported to the middle of the most beautiful scenery in Europe, as he rightly called it. Paul Potts was unusual in being both one of Orwell's drinking friends, whom his family and others disliked, but one well up to making his way to Jura. The explanation was, of course, that he came from Canada and these distances seemed as slight to him as they did to Orwell.

The time came when Potts and the others, even Inez, went back to their ordinary lives. There remained Orwell's family and a few friends of a more serious kind. Most important was Richard Rees, Orwell's publisher, who soon realised that the idea of Orwell running a croft by himself based on Barnhill was impracticable. He saw that with some help it should be possible for a living to be made and he decided to add some of his capital to the meagre amount available to Orwell. Although *Animal Farm* was doing well it did not appear in America until August 1946, after which Orwell could draw on effectively unlimited sums, after the usual lapse between royalties being earned and paid. Rees himself could not be of much use on a farm. He spent his time either talking with Orwell or painting views nearby. Orwell attempted to do some work on the book but it amounted to little more than the work he did at his cottage before the war but with greater difficulty because of his failing health and the tendency of the deer to eat anything that had been planted as soon as it appeared. The Fletchers at Ardlussa soon provided an answer and a refreshing breath of fresh air into the Blair household.

Bill Dunn had returned from the war lacking one leg but still hale and hearty and eager to get down to work, preferably on the land. He placed an advertisement in the *Oban Times* asking if anyone had a small croft or farm that he could become involved with and the Fletchers saw this and replied. He was soon living on Jura at Kenuachdrach and shortly after moved down into Barnhill to work the land full-time. He had another reason for moving—his affection for Orwell's sister Avril which soon blossomed into a firm relationship which was, perhaps, the most surprising and certainly the most long-lasting of the results of Orwell's decision to go to Jura. In the end it was Bill Dunn and Avril who brought up Richard, rather than Orwell's second wife Sonia; Orwell's decision, worked out with Eileen, did create for his son a life which he would have wanted him to live, although he died when the boy was so young.

The farm began to prosper in the short term. Orwell wrote a letter to David Astor during his second long stay on the island describing the progress which had by then taken place. Sheep and cattle had appeared, some bought with Orwell's money, and also a pig. Orwell remarked to Astor jokingly, in the context of *Animal Farm*, that he was not happy with the animal and that he was glad it was being fattened up to be turned into bacon at the earliest opportunity. It was in many ways an idyllic life contrasting as starkly as possible with the acute cold of the winter of 1947 in London, worse even than the previous year. Orwell would have been better advised to stay on Jura but he returned to London and only made a short return visit in the early new year. The summer of 1947 made up for the winter. It was exceedingly hot and Orwell went on expeditions over to the other side of the island where there were caves and extensive beaches and no people at all.

This year he had with him more of his family rather than the literary assembly that met in 1946. Gwen O'Shaugnessy came with her children and the Dakins (Orwell's elder sister had married Dakin) who became involved in an adventure with real danger when Orwell misjudged the times of the tides by the famous Corryvrecken whirlpool. Henry Dakin, his sister Jane, Orwell and Richard were caught in the whirlpool. Their boat lost its outboard motor and only by the merest luck and strong rowing by Dakin they landed on a small island, no more than a strip of land barely rising above the water where they were picked up by a lobster boat that happened to be passing. Orwell had many close shaves in his life but this was perhaps the closest. The accident was soon forgotten as the days passed, but beneath the happiness of the idyllic summer other problems began to emerge.

Orwell worked consistently on *Nineteen Eighty-Four* through his second year on Jura, with breaks for his fishing excursions, but his health did not improve. It deteriorated through the autumn and with the onset of winter he suffered a relapse which could not be covered up. As in Cologne, which must have seemed an age away, he had a haemorrhage but this time he had to go to a sanatorium near Glasgow where they had no hesitation in diagnosing tuberculosis. He spent six months there only returning to Jura the follow July. Many warned him not to, but looking back on his life now, it is obvious that he counted every day of his life since Cologne (when he drew up his will and literary executor's notes) as a day won against the odds. He wanted more than anything to finish *Nineteen Eighty-Four* and the book was inextricably tied up with his life on Jura. If we value the book he created then we have to respect the way he chose to write it. Had he gone back to London he would never have finished the book at all. He made the point clearly and forcefully in letters to friends and it was the weekly journalism—and no doubt the political fighting behind it—which he thought would make work impossible. The paucity of work produced by the people around him in London at that time, nothing at all compared to *Nineteen Eighty-Four*, shows again how right he was.

The second long summer on Jura was clouded by more than just his health. Bill Dunn now says clearly that the farm simply could not run at a profit without continual input of capital either from Richard Rees or someone else. He subsequently moved to the mainland and experienced completely different conditions where an economic life was possible; he referred to Jura later as a waste by comparison. It is no chance that the deer on the island out-numbered the people by twenty-five to one and that barely a handful of crofts actually support the people working on them. Compton Mackenzie's dream would be possible, but only for people prepared to live at a low standard of living. Jura never had 10,000 population as Orwell thought: 2000 was the highest and then people lived in extreme poverty as the few surviving croft buildings from that era show. People lived off seaweed as a staple element in their diet—sheep and deer still eat it today; it is an unusual sight to see them grazing, particularly the deer—and it is possible to incorporate it into bread. Only for the few years Orwell lived on the island was the standard of living comparable to that on the mainland, and that was because of the wartime shortages and rationing. The end of it all was that Orwell's dream was over, although he left the island for the last time some while

before Bill Dunn and Avril took Richard and decided to leave
for the mainland.

Perhaps the best understanding of what Jura meant to
Orwell can be found in the private letters he wrote to his
friends and acquaintances. The post was irregular, at best
twice a week, but he managed to keep in touch with most of
the people who mattered to him, telling all of them something
about the life he was living often with detailed instructions
for a journey which, he often repeated, need take little more
than two days. Writing to Celia Goodman, he described his
night-time lobster fishing expeditions, explaining that he had
mastered the art of tying lobsters' claws—very dangerous it
seems, 'especially when you have to do it in the dark'. At one
point David Astor gave the Orwells a pony which did not
want to take the shafts of the trap it was meant to pull and
so was ridden about, to save petrol, on less important tasks.
The snag was that it was very tiring riding bareback and this
produced a characteristic letter to Anthony Powell:

> Have you got or do you know anyone who has got a saddle
> for sale? Good condition doesn't matter very much so long
> it has a sound girth and stirrups. It's for a horse only about
> 14 h[ands] but on the stout side, so very likely a saddle
> belonging to a big horse would do. It's the sort of thing
> someone might have kicking around & you can't buy them
> for love or money.

Whether Powell found one is not recorded. The contrast
between such needs and the life lived in England by people
such as Powell was acute, and there is a sneaking suspicion
that Orwell wrote with his request partly to pull Powell's leg.
This idea comes over even more strongly when he talks of the
disadvantages of life on the island in winter: 'Part of the winter
may be pretty bleak and one is sometimes cut off from the
mainland for a week or two but it doesn't matter so long as
you have flour in hand to make scones'. This was the sort of
homely real world detail that Orwell revelled in and which

made the London sophisticated literary *beau monde* shudder, as Orwell surely knew it would. One letter, giving detailed instructions to Sonia for the journey to Barnhill, perhaps intending to be as accurate as possible, succeeded in making it sound like a full-scale expedition. The final note was an urgent request that the time she intended leaving should be forwarded well in advance since the hire of a private car was an essential part of the journey and as there were only two posts and Orwell went into Craighouse at most twice a week, where the car had to be hired (there was no phone at either Barnhill or Ardlussa—there still isn't at Barnhill) it was essential that he get to Craighouse to order the car well in advance. These tortuous directions contrast sharply with his delighted recounting of his own travels to and from the island: 'the journeys one makes are quite astonishing' he remarked over one escapade going to fetch Susan Watson's daughter from Glasgow which, because of a missed ferry connection, ended up taking three days, in colonial terms the time it took to go by train from the north of India to Madras.

What came over in the end was his deep attachment to the island which had developed over those two summers. In no fewer than three letters in August and September 1947 he said that they were all going to stay the winter in Jura, because the weather was milder, if more damp, and there were less leaks in the roof at Barnhill than in his London flat. Food was more readily available too. But really he wanted to stay for the simple reason that he dreaded what was waiting for him in London, as he said, again to Anthony Powell: 'We are planning to spend the winter here, because I can get on with my work without getting constantly bogged down in journalism.' Jura had become his home.

Orwell did not stay that winter on Jura because he had another relapse. He returned only once more and then began the steady progression from one sanatorium to another as his condition deteriorated, going finally to a ward in University College Hospital, London, where he was to die. When Richard

153

visited him there with Bill and Avril there was never any question of them all moving back to London; Jura was his and their home. It surely must have been the difficulty of life after the war that prevented Orwell being buried in the cemetery at Inverlussa where all the others who lived on the estate were buried, including Robin Fletcher whom he had got to know so well in writing his book, as we shall see. Visitors who make the journey to Jura, even if they do not get as far as Barnhill, will perhaps feel Orwell by them, even if he lies buried in England.

CHAPTER FOURTEEN

Jura, Japan and the writing of
Nineteen Eighty-Four

There is still some mystery about how Orwell came actually to live on Jura, rather than simply visiting for a while, staying with some old crofters of great age as David Astor thought he was going to do. He has stated later, quite clearly, that there was no question of Orwell actually going to live on Jura as far as he was concerned. This seems to be borne out by the absence of any reference to him at the time, or that he visited Orwell. Paul Potts' talk of the wealthy neighbour with shooting-brakes would seem to refer to Astor, for the Fletchers were not that kind of laird, and Orwell's insistence that they carry their own burdens, when it was obvious help could have been sought, suggests that he specifically did not seek a close link at the time.

The Fletchers were quite different. Robin Fletcher had been a school master at Eton before the war and had only just come to Jura after being in a Japanese concentration camp and working on the Burma Road. The Ardlussa estate was actually his wife's which she had inherited as we have seen when her last brother had been killed. After time recuperating he began creating a small community at Ardlussa that was not unlike the kind of community Orwell himself had originally envisaged. Apart from signing an agreement with Richard Rees and Bill Dunn to run the farm around Barnhill, he brought other people to the estate and saw a small pottery come into existence. In the end he came to realise, as Bill Dunn did, that the venture could not support itself without outside help. It was no accident that so many of the lairds had sold to wealthy landowners—the Ardlussa estate had been bought by the Browns (from the banking firm of Brown Shipley) in just this way. The present generation of Fletchers have turned once again to the deer, improving the stock immeasurably and experimenting with new forms of fish farming. In Orwell's day things were different, and the key figure whom Orwell got to know well was Robin Fletcher.

It has been said that neither Orwell nor Robin Fletcher knew that they had a common background before they met. This seems unlikely, particularly in view of the widespread knowledge that Orwell was a pseudonym for Eric Blair amongst old Etonians as we have seen. However within a short time of Orwell's arriving he would have discovered who Robin Fletcher was and his very strong family connection with Eton. He was a nephew of Charles R. L. Fletcher, the biographer of the famous Eton headmaster Edmonde Warre, and in the library at Ardlussa were Charles Fletcher's own copies of his biography and the bulk of his library all bearing his bookplate. It is hardly surprising that Orwell began to have lengthy talks with Robin Fletcher, all the more because they shared as well a common experience of the Far East, Orwell in Burma as an administrator and Fletcher as a prisoner of war, virtually a slave, working on the Burma Road. This connection is of direct importance for *Nineteen Eighty-Four* and helps explain what seems at first to be a weakness of the book, commented on by many critics, the excessive violence of the scenes in 'Room 101'.

The ravages that work on the Burma Road wrought on those put to work on it are now almost accepted in an age of endless starvation brought into our living rooms by television nightly. At the end of the war the newsreels showing Englishmen and people from the colonies as they were released from the Japanese camps created a profound sense of horror. In those days there were no 'after care' facilities and when the men came home they were simply taken to their families, as Robin Fletcher was. Orwell's descriptions of Winston being reduced to a near-skeletal form were a reality for the Fletchers and many families like them, not just footage on newsreels seen in crowded cinemas. The bitterness against the Japanese has lasted with most of the families affected to the present day, despite all that has happened since, and rightly so. The revelations of the concentration camps were horrific also; they went to show that such things were possible in Europe, indeed worse things, for the Japanese seem never to have actually exterminated their enemies by the million. But they simply drew people's attention away from the tens of thousands who had died or been reduced to unrecognisable skeletal beings by their time in the camps. This seems to have been the case particularly in the literary world, at least as far as the critics of the violence of Room 101 are concerned. They saw Winston's condition, so closely resembling that of Robin Fletcher and all the others on their release, as being nothing more than a symptom of Orwell's own medical condition. In one extreme case Anthony West (no relation of the present author) described at length how Orwell's book was a reversion to childhood fears and persecutions and a psychological document from start to finish.

There are a few details in *Nineteen Eighty-Four* which seem to have come from the same source. One is unimportant, but so strange as to have defied rational explanation until now: the drink which all outer party members consume is Victory Gin. Orwell describes Winston drinking it, bracing himself for the impact as he drank it at one gulp. Orwell describes its odour: 'It gave off a sickly, oily smell as of Chinese rice-spirit.' This drink would have been well known to Orwell and to Fletcher—it was the cheaply produced native drink which performed the same function as cheap

157

gin anywhere. No doubt the guards on the Burma Road drank it, and perhaps their captives if they were lucky. Another detail was more serious, the final torture in Room 101. Winston Smith is told that he will have a cage fitted over his head which has in it two starving rats. When a door inside the cage is opened they will fly straight at his face and eat into it. The cage is brought close enough for him to smell the animals, when O'Brien remarks: 'It was a common punishment in Imperial China'. *Nineteen Eighty-Four* features prisoners from Eastasia, and there is a passage in the original draft manuscript referring to crimes committed by the Eastasians but there is no actual reference to explain why China should appear in these two trivial details unless through Orwell's memory of them from his days in Burma, and, perhaps, from talking with Robin Fletcher about what life was like out there, with the Japanese effectively taking over from China and absorbing it, and everything else in their path.

Orwell was afraid that totalitarianism could come to Britain and saw his book as a warning against what *might* happen; but what could have led him to think that the sufferings that Fletcher and his comrades in arms had suffered could ever come to Britain? The immediate explanation that springs to mind is that Orwell in Burma was *not* a prisoner, but one of the ruling caste, from an alien civilisation. There was never any question of Orwell torturing prisoners of course but Mulk Raj Anand, who visited Orwell on Jura, said Orwell was well aware that native troops could resort to time-honoured methods when getting information they wanted. This knowledge only helped to make him more determined than ever to bring about Indian independence and put an end to the colonial system. But again, was there any reason for thinking that such things could happen *in Britain*, that people in Britain could be brought to the state where they could torture each other in the way that Winston Smith was tortured, using methods more appropriate to a Third World autocracy than the home of democracy? Orwell knew from his experience in Spain and what he saw in Germany that inhumanity on this scale was all too possible, even though the ordinary Englishman would find it unthinkable. Orwell believed that it *was* unthinkable for the real Englishman and that such cruelty was alien to everything that England meant to him. But there had been changes in the twentieth century in Britain as well.

Censorship in modern Britain began during the Boer War and has been shown to have stemmed largely from fears of the concentration camps and their appalling death tolls becoming known in Britain. People such as Sir Wilfrid Lawson fought against the evil that this interference with free speech created but without success. The corruption of British public morals that he foresaw came to pass and the English character now, with its political police and quasi-totalitarian systems—all be it forced on the country by two world wars—is totally different from what it was. Orwell was essentially fighting the same fight and he knew instinctively that if censorship of the kind he had experienced was possible then anything was possible.

There have been very few concentration camps on British soil. They are little known, understandably, as the worst of them were in the Channel Islands when they were under German control. The only camps, properly so-called on English soil and under English control in peace time were the camps for German refugees at Richborough in Kent, just before the war. The regime there was mild in the extreme and they could scarcely be called concentration camps in the sense the word subsequently came to have. They were run by the Society for German Jewry and, although jokingly referred to by those coming to them as *Anglo-saxonhausen*, its purposes were benevolent. This camp speedily gave way to the ordinary detention camps for those held under 18b after war broke out. Orwell never explicitly condemns these camps or detention without trial on political grounds although he spoke about the agitation against the release of Sir Oswald Mosley as being

159

wrong. Neither does he comment on the 'tough' interrogation centre at Ham Common although, since he followed the parliamentary debates either in person or through Hansard, he would have known what went on there.

The importance for *Nineteen Eighty-Four* of whether Orwell knew of Ham Common is considerable. The parliamentary reports are quite specific about the conditions under which men were detained. These included being kept awake for lengthy periods under bright lights in cells that were so small that it was not possible to sit properly. Anyone reading the accounts, and any of the unpublished accounts of the regime there cannot help but be struck by the resemblance between them and Orwell's description of the cells in the Ministry of Love. The medical consultant at Ham Common, when asked what the purpose of this treatment was, replied: 'To bring about a state of unreserved loquacity', and Orwell's description of the behaviour of those in the cell with Winston show exactly this being achieved. The existence of Ham Common was known only to a few and Orwell seems never to have mentioned it—even if he had done so in one of his articles it would not have reached print. However once again there are signs that Orwell knew a considerable amount about both 18b detention centres and the political police—MI5—which he was undoubtedly caricaturing in his brilliant creation of 'the Thought Police'.

The idea that his creation Room 101 might have the same root as the Thought Police, and that they might have led him to fear the appearance of the kind of treatment Robin Fletcher and the others experienced in Burma in England, is a valid one and can be seen by tracing the signs showing his actual knowledge of MI5, ending finally at the suggestion that he himself worked as an agent for the security service. The first explicit reference worth noticing occurs in an article written just after the Labour Party had come to power:

When a Labour Government takes over, I wonder what

happens to Scotland Yard Special Branch? To Military Intelligence? To the Consular Service? . . . We are not told, but such symptoms as there are do not suggest that any very extensive reshuffling is going on. We are still represented by the same ambassadors and the BBC censorship seems to have the same subtly reactionary colour it always had.

The article was called 'Freedom of the Park' and concerned the case of five news-vendors who were charged with obstruction for trying to sell their papers—pacifist papers for the most part. Orwell clearly wondered why this had been done and remarked mischievously that a Labour government was in power, not the wartime administration. His references to Special Branch and MI5 would probably not have passed the censor during the war so Orwell took the opportunity to mention them knowing that the detention and prosecution of people for political reasons would have to involve them. It might have also occurred to him that the people detained were enemies of the Communist Party too. His mentioning censorship of the BBC in the same context points to his most important area of knowledge of the political police in Britain. The BBC during the war had every appointment vetted by MI5 (indeed the process went on for some years after the war and in a modified form still does). Orwell had practical experience of its working when he tried to get Mulk Raj Anand a full-time job with the Indian service. All his attempts failed and Orwell felt very badly about this as he and Eileen were very close to Anand and his wife, and later their daughter, Orwell's god-daughter. The reason was that the 'college' (as the vetting by MI5 was referred to) would not pass Anand. One day Anand pressed Orwell very hard for the reason and a short while later Orwell showed him a file saying that he could see from what was in it why they could never accept him. Anand remarked:

It had a list of every meeting I had attended, every

161

communist colleague I knew and so on; I could see what he meant.

The odd thing about this is that no such file could possibly be held by the BBC itself. At best it must have been given Orwell by the MI5 liaison officer within the BBC, which raises the question of what Orwell was doing being on such close terms with the Thought Police themselves. There was another case involving one of his Indian broadcasters who spoke Gujerati. MI5 discovered he had a dubious past, politically-speaking, and he was removed. Unfortunately the man who took his place had been so long away from India that he was no longer fluent in his dialect. For six months the banned speaker carried on doing the programme, splitting the fee with his friend. One can imagine the amusement this must have caused Orwell and the consternation amongst the 'college'.

Beyond this experience we have already seen Eileen's work and the contact it gave her with MI5's work on surveillance of political organisations through the mail and press. Telephone tapping was also widely known about in the days when the telephone system and the postal system were run by the same national company. Orwell would have known of this but also known the more 'public' side of MI5's work, namely gossip in Cyril Connolly's circle and the open bragging of MI5 contacts by people such as Kingsley Martin. When Burgess defected most of his friends disowned him but some, such as Cyril Connolly, wrote about that circle in the Cafe Royal with some objectivity. Burgess indeed got close to Orwell but with what purpose is not clear—he only used Orwell once in espionage terms by getting him to arrange a meeting with Stafford Cripps, which Orwell was able to do. Knowledge of these various worlds did not imply any likely involvement, far from it. But there were two clear links with the real world of spies in the early days of the war. The first was through his contemporary at Eton, Christopher Hollis. Hollis had looked him up when he was in Burma, and Orwell kept in touch with him when he returned. There are a number of coded references to their meetings, for example when Orwell remarked that 'he had it on good authority' that the figures for the Battle of Britain were reasonably accurate. This was a reference to Christopher Hollis who was at that time in Air Force Intelligence; Orwell's comment was not much of a leak more of an indiscretion unless, indeed, it was an officially inspired leak. The significance of this Hollis connection is that Roger Hollis, Christopher's brother, was the case officer for the Communist Party, Claud Cockburn, the *Daily Worker* at the time of its suppression, and so on. Orwell became deeply involved in the struggle against the People's Convention as we have seen. He did not give the name of the man who thought the danger of the Convention underestimated so we have no way of knowing whether it was Christopher Hollis or not, but one thing is clear and that is Orwell would very likely have come to the attention of MI5 through his activities at this time even if he was not already known to them through his Spain file. And his remarks that it was held against a man to have fought in Spain, even when asking to go on an ordinary job, suggests that he was known to MI5 because of this and knew it. Roger Hollis was by no means obliging to the Security Executive in putting down the *Daily Worker* and indeed successfully concealed from his superiors that he was a close personal friend of Cockburn's as he remained right through his life. He might well have reacted with annoyance against Orwell and his activities, and indeed would seem to have had a diametrically opposed view of life to his brother Christopher. The reader can begin to see from this the feeling Winston Smith has of never knowing who was in the Thought Police and who was not, only ever knowing for sure when he was arrested by one, the keeper of the antique shop where Winston and Julia meet.

The vague connections here prove nothing, but there was another link, the second person, who quite definitely was a member of MI5. One of Orwell's colleagues in 1940 is now known to have been a close personal friend of Maxwell Knight's. His friendship, which had a perfectly respectable cover, carried on for long after the war and, when the author spoke with him, it became obvious that Orwell occupied a similar position in his world. The reason for the author pursuing this connection was a simple one: a retired CIA officer in Washington had frankly said that Orwell worked for MI5. Whether the statement was mischievous, or a mistake, or the kind of thing a retired 'spook' habitually says about anyone named who was at all famous was not clear, but the statement was positive and not withdrawn. There can only be circumstantial evidence of such a connection unless MI5 records are opened but Maxwell Knight was well known for running an outstation from his flat in Dolphin Square that was largely unaccountable. If it was he that Orwell knew or worked through, only one of a few other agents would have known about the connection. The circumstantial evidence in *Nineteen Eighty-Four* is slight: O'Brien in the original draft has a pseudonym and tells Winston and Julia that they will have to have one as well—Maxwell Knight used many cover names and always insisted others used them as well. Hollis also used other names, indeed the whole panoply of secrecy of 'the Brotherhood' sounds like conventional security practice as Maxwell Knight would have known it. The flat that Winston and Julia go to bears again a strong resemblance to the luxury flat that Knight lived in. Other fragments pointing to a connection are such things as Orwell possessing (besides a service revolver on Jura) a small black automatic, standard issue for the security service.

The clutching at straws, the suspicion, almost the persecution mania, or paranoia that these speculations resemble are exactly the kind of worries Winston Smith and all the members of the outer party have in *Nineteen Eighty-Four*, and they were worries which were inevitable with the introduction of a Thought Police, as Sir Wilfrid Lawson foresaw. But what if Orwell was indeed someone working for Knight, and with a woman fellow agent? We can only speculate on who he was reporting on and why—perhaps Burgess was fighting Orwell at the BBC because he knew through Blunt or another mole that Orwell had security service connections. Orwell, a man who stood for truth and honesty would have to become almost a split personality unless he believed profoundly in what he was doing—to the point of acting in a way which went against all his professed opinions. In an unpublished letter to Rayner Heppenstal he once said that he thought Judas Iscariot had had a bad press, and the creation of a character such as O'Brien, the leader of the revolutionary cell who is actually on Big Brother's side would, if Orwell *was* betraying his beliefs by spying on people, be a way of examining his own position, and the same goes for the shop-keeper. And betrayal and doublethink would suddenly have an entirely new meaning if Orwell was guilty of such betrayal of his own ideals.

In the calm isolation of Jura this kind of thinking, as much part of the London world he left as the political bickering, would soon have evaporated. In talking to Robin Fletcher he would have found the real effect of the totalitarian systems of thought that the English Marxists found so attractive. It may have been that at one time he inflicted torture indirectly on subject races, as, in some kind of cross-racial revenge, the Japanese had inflicted intolerable hardships on their European prisoners. It may have been that, if he had become involved with Maxwell Knight or his friends in their struggles against the communists in London—and Knight fought against them when everyone else took the side of Russia, Philby and Burgess with the rest—he was deceiving people around him. But he knew that he rejected imperialism and had done so in a way that completely altered his life, and he rejected political police and all their wiles, and would show it in his book. The Thought Police is a brilliant satirical idea. It seems to have evolved in the actual process of writing the book on Jura, for there was no reference to it in the original outline which has survived from 1943. Other elements in *Nineteen Eighty-Four* which do not appear in the first notes include the Brotherhood and Big Brother, all references to atomic war, unimagined in 1943, and a large number of incidental details such as the execution of war criminals which were drawn into his satire as the book was being written. The chance survival of a number of his drafts of the book in various stages has enabled the evolution of the book to be studied, and a fairly accurate idea of exactly how the book finally emerged is possible. The picture drawn is an unpleasant one of struggle and exhaustion; like Robin Fletcher, Orwell must have been extremely glad to have got away from such an awful past, to find himself living in one of the most beautiful parts of Europe. However painful the memory or the act of creation there was always, through the window, the Sound of Jura.

CHAPTER FIFTEEN

Orwell and the Atomic Bomb

Nineteen Eighty-Four is set in a post-atomic war Britain, and yet the reader only realises this when he is directly told of it. There are no signs in the world Orwell describes that there has been such a war, no radiation, no post-Hiroshima scenario of horrific injuries and total destruction. This has led some critics to accuse Orwell of ignoring the bomb and the issues which it raised, or of failing to understand something of such immense significance so soon after the event. The bomb was not mentioned in the original outline and was not thought of, even, in the time between his original plotting of the book and the complete destruction of Hiroshima and Nagasaki. Orwell's bland reference to atomic wars in the fifties and the dropping of an atomic bomb on Colchester seems to show a complete lack of understanding of the forces involved which even calls into doubt the entire book's validity. Actually Orwell was fully conscious of the threat of nuclear war and the scenario he develops was a result of careful thought about the society that was likely to result from the existence of such weapons. His vision of a totalitarian society perpetuated for ever was in direct contrast to views on the problem put forward by people such as John Middleton Murry, Orwell's original publisher, and other political figures.

Orwell's first response to the atomic bomb was an essay 'You and the Atom Bomb' which appeared in *Tribune* for 19 October, 1945. It raised first a question which showed how little was really known about the bomb in those days. It was thought that the great secrecy surrounding the bomb and its manufacture was because the process was not expensive. It was thought that if the secret got out then anyone could rapidly make the bomb, if not an individual then certainly a country. We have only now reached that stage, with fears that Saddam Hussein might get the bomb. It was soon realised that only a very few countries could possibly envisage making the bomb and the idea that large numbers of petty dictators could plunge the world into nuclear war was wrong. Orwell's next suggestion was very close to what actually happened:

But suppose—and this is really the likeliest development—that the surviving great nations make a tacit agreement never to use the atomic bomb against one another? Suppose they only use it, or the threat of it against people who are unable to retaliate? In that case we are back to where we were before [i.e. before the appearance of the bomb], the only difference being that power is concentrated in still fewer hands and the outlook for subject peoples and oppressed classes is still more hopeless.

The idea that America or Russia or Britain might actually use the bomb against smaller countries indicates how little the immense power of the weapon had permeated people's thinking. Orwell appears to have realised nothing about radiation or its dangers; certainly he never mentions it. He envisages the use of a bomb against smaller countries and can envisage a bomb falling on Colchester without any other bomb falling, and with life in London going on much as before. And yet his underlying understanding was sound. The split of the world into great superpowers, which gave him the ideas for both *Animal Farm* and *Nineteen Eighty-Four*, was confirmed by the threat of nuclear war, although it was a threat levelled at the superpowers themselves—if they made a tacit agreement it was not in evidence at the time of the Cuba incident. The initial optimism in this article has gone by the time he came to write *Nineteen Eighty-Four*, and he assumes that the tacit agreement had failed and that war had occurred. Beyond that war he assumed a stalemate would occur and that there would be established slave-states that might last for millennia, like the old slave empires whose relics can now be seen in the British Museum, and in sites far off in the deserts in the Middle East. Orwell ended his essay with a touch of the kind of humour which appealed to the readers of his column, and which had within it very shrewd analysis of a problem:

> Had the atomic bomb turned out to be something as cheap and easily manufactured as a bicycle or an alarm clock it might well have plunged us back into barbarism, but it might on the other hand, have meant the end of national sovereignty and of the highly-centralised police state. If, as seems to be the case, it is a rare and costly object as difficult to produce as a battle-ship, it is likelier to put an end to large-scale wars at the cost of prolonging indefinitely a 'peace that is no peace'.

The expense of building a nuclear bomb was of course far greater than that of building a mere battle-ship and Orwell's analogy here reflects the immensity of the project and even his inability to grasp what was involved. His analysis nevertheless is extremely accurate, and a 'peace that is no peace' is precisely what the world has had in the half-century since the war ended. The highly-centralised police state which Orwell saw as surviving *did* survive in the East epitomised by the Stasi. And who is to say that Orwell's warning in *Nineteen Eighty-Four* was not a significant factor in the failure of such a regime, at least in that form, to be established in Britain?

In the same essay Orwell actually tied in one of the key phrases that was to dominate political analysis through the following decades, whilst explaining that he was concerned with:

. . . the kind of beliefs and the social structure that would probably prevail in a state which was at once *unconquerable* and in a permanent state of 'cold war' with its neighbours.

Orwell was not the only person struggling with such problems. One of the writers who was also concerned and publishing a great deal at the time was, once again, John Middleton Murry. Despite their differences earlier in the war they came to share some common ground, mainly because of a correspondence initiated by Murry in 1944 that took Orwell to task for attacking his kind of pacifism. Orwell replied by saying that the pacifists, Murry foremost amongst them, had proposed pacifism in the West but been indifferent about the question in the East. Nothing had been said about Russia, Orwell pointed out, despite all that happened there; Murry was indeed, in a phrase which Orwell himself rejected later, objectively pro-Stalin. Murry had replied in his turn to explain that he had changed his views, particularly about Stalin. This produced one of Orwell's characteristic letters immediately admitting his fault:

I must apologise very deeply for attacking you on the score of your attitude to the USSR. I seldom see *Peace News* and did not know that you had taken this line . . . I ought to have kept up with your utterances and I am very sorry that I have written you an almost abusive letter founded on out-of-date information. I know only too well what sort of trouble it gets one into to write anything anti-Stalin at this date, and I admire your courage in doing so.

There are few who would write such a candid reply; it was from acts such as this that Orwell's reputation for honesty stemmed. It is clear from this that Orwell followed Murry's opinions closely from then on, and we know that he received a copy of Murry's book *The Free Society* because he wrote acknowledging it with comments from his hospital bed, as we shall see, and we know that he kept it because the book survives in the Orwell archive, with what may well be Orwell's markings in it. The fact that Orwell had the book, as he also had his earlier manifesto (referred to in chapter ten) *The Brotherhood of Peace* is important because it establishes the likelihood of certain influences on Orwell in Murry's work which otherwise might be less certain. The main idea was that of Brotherhood. The Brotherhood appears in *Nineteen Eighty-Four* as an underground movement with very much the mores of the Christian pacifists who urged the slaughter of 20,000 Eurasian prisoners. But this is, of course, an aspect of the satire. The concept of Brotherhood was much discussed at the time when any intellectual of sensibility was trying to establish, as Orwell was, the kinds of belief and social structure that would prevail in the post-war world. In a review of Arthur Koestler's *The Yogi and the Commissar* he described Koestler's point that practical men—the inventors of the atom bomb—had led mankind to the edge of an abyss but the intellectuals 'in whom acceptance of power politics has killed first the moral sense, then the sense of reality . . .' were still pushing forward, blind to the possible consequences. Koestler went on to call for a new fraternity and Orwell quotes him directly:

". . . a new fraternity in a spiritual climate, whose leaders are tied by a vow of poverty to share the life of the masses, and debarred by the laws of the fraternity from attaining unchecked power" and he adds: "If this seems Utopian, then socialism is a Utopia."

Orwell's creation of a Big Brother suggests the way he thought such laws would prove useless and that a Stalin or Hitler would always appear.

The religious element in *Nineteen Eighty-Four* has already been mentioned. The concept of Brotherhood was of course a basic idea common to all Christians and the suggestion

171

of a fraternity in that spirit was also made at the time. Eileen's friend, the novelist Lettice Cooper, referred to the 'brotherhood of man' as being the only very general religion available at the time. As with most religious ideas of this kind brotherhood also acquired a political dimension. It was a leading idea for all Christian socialists and there had actually been a Brotherhood Movement which really existed at the end of the nineteenth century. It appeared at about the same time as Drage's lecture at Eton on the social question and its manifesto, written by John Coleman Kenworthy, was called *From Bondage to Brotherhood: A Message to the Workers*. It published a weekly newspaper, *Brotherhood*, and survived until nearly the end of World War I. It reappeared briefly in the thirties before finally becoming amalgamated with the Peace Pledge Union. It may well be that Middleton Murry knew of the movement from that connection; the idea of brotherhood certainly inspired his pamphlet, *The Brotherhood of Peace*, and featured prominently in *The Free Society* but in an entirely new and original phase, connected directly with the need to control the new atomic weapons.

For a brief period after the war America was the sole producer of the atomic bomb. After the two bombs dropped on Japan it was obvious that the history of mankind had entered a new phase. As Orwell remarked 'It is a commonplace that the history of civilisation is largely the history of weapons'. Although America seemed to have the advantage over Russia it did not act as though it did, and we now know that the Soviet spies had ensured that it was only a matter of time before Russia too had the bomb. At this period a suggestion was put forward by Bernard Baruch, known as the Baruch Proposals, that there should be an Atomic Authority, to be established by the United Nations as 'a supra-National body having complete control and full possession of the means to produce atomic energy throughout the world, and not subject to the veto-power of the Security Council'.

It was realised that this suggestion would create a group

of men who would have the power of life and death over the world. At the time Murry was writing the Atomic Authority was a real possibility; it was only the Russians' rejection that ended the idea (and this is the real damage done by the atom spies, now completely lost sight of). He rapidly developed his own idea of what kind of men these keepers of the world's future would be. He asked the question *Quis custodiet ipsos custodes?* And the further obvious question of how anyone could be sure they would act for the world's good.

> The question takes us to the heart of the proposal. It appears to make the Utopian demand that the personnel of the Atomic Authority shall be a band of brothers, with the unity of a religious order.

The continuity of Murry's thought can be seen by comparing this with a quotation from his manifesto, *The Brotherhood of Peace:*

> We are a band of brothers committed to the exploration of a new world. We have entered into a new spiritual dimension; and, however much we may shrink from the phrase, we are already members of a new religious fraternity.

We cannot know whether Orwell made this comparison, but he had both texts by him. Although he had made his peace with Murry in 1944 he seems to have had no doubt that the ideas in the 1940 pamphlet, directly resembling the ideas in *The Free Society* concerning a completely different world with its actual destruction imminent, were wrong, as the later proposals were wrong. In each case the band of brothers would have a Big Brother who would rise to the top. And with atomic power he would exert an absolute tyranny. Orwell did not believe there would be a global power but two or three superpowers, each with the bomb, and that the tyranny would be proper to each of the powers which would not interfere with the others after seeing, perhaps, the consequences of one atomic war of limited extent—the bomb on Colchester. The only question then was which of the superpowers Britain would belong to if she relinquished her role as head of the old Empire, and how they would get hold of Britain. That such a scenario was possible, Orwell firmly believed: he saw that possibility in 1943 and he saw it all the more strongly in 1946 and after, when he was writing his book. The danger came from infiltration of the British Labour Party by the Communist Party, the subject of much debate at the time. The attempted coup intended to replace Attlee immediately after the election was won, in which Burgess's friend, and later Chairman of the Labour Party, Maurice Webb, was much involved, was only the first move of the kind. Once that had happened then the inner party would take over. Opposition would be dealt with through *agents provocateur* and other such moves—just as O'Brien leads Winston Smith and Julia into the Brotherhood. They never seem to realise that Big Brother must surely be at the head of the movement that bears his name.

The suggestion that Ingsoc in *Nineteen Eighty-Four* is *specifically* derived from an amalgamation of the Communist Party and the Labour Party would until recently have been seen as mischievous speculation. However the publication of the extant manuscript of Orwell's book has established that this was the basis for his invention, for an earlier draft clearly states it. The survival of this manuscript is an extremely fortunate chance for anyone interested in the development of Orwell's masterpiece. The actual development of his thought whilst he worked at Barnhill on Jura can be followed in considerable detail. Not only can we see evolution of ideas such as Ingsoc but the appalling labour of working under the intense strain caused by his illness is clear to us. In the rest of this chapter some of the differences in theme and detail that are revealed by the manuscript will be considered, including the story of the actual survival of these papers, for they are not really the 'extant manuscript' except in the most literal sense.

The Extant Manuscript

The arrival of the year 1984 itself created such intense publishing interest in Orwell's work that it was decided to publish a facsimile of what has become known as the extant manuscript. The history of this manuscript is easily told. Some time after Orwell's death Sonia Orwell came to Barnhill and went through the papers that had survived there in the room where Orwell did most of his typing. Amongst these papers she found what appeared to be the manuscript for *Nineteen Eighty-Four*. She preserved this for a while and then sent it to a Red Cross charity auction without having made any examination of it other than to verify its general nature. The auctioneers sold it simply as the original manuscript without comment. In a letter to the final owner Sonia Orwell said that she knew the manuscript was imperfect, although not quite as imperfect as it subsequently proved to be. It was obvious from her remarks that she failed completely to understand what the typescript she found in her husband's room actually was.

The reality of the situation was that the manuscript was actually a group of rejected drafts, the material from which Orwell extracted the final version of the book and on which he spent the last ounces of his energy at Barnhill. The actual manuscript of *Nineteen Eighty-Four* was effectively identical with the published text and survives at the Orwell archive.

For scholars and enthusiasts for Orwell's work the publication of the manuscript, indeed its survival, provides a unique opportunity to study the evolution of one of the most important works of fiction published this century. This kind of survival is rare because the drafts of texts, the author's working copy, are usually destroyed. Any surviving working draft is interesting because it shows the evolution of an author's ideas. There are here shifts of emphasis, themes that have been dropped from the final book and details that have been altered, all bearing on the roots of *Nineteen Eighty-Four*. A detailed account of all that is to be found in the facsimile reproduction will have to await final analysis of the paper upon which Orwell wrote his articles and letters as well as the drafts since it will only then be possible to tell in exactly what order the various drafts and amendments were written. However, just as it has been possible to look at two areas that were not in the first draft—atomic warfare and the Brotherhood movement—so a number of interesting changes can be found in the text from what is clearly evident in the draft, in whatever order it was written. The period between the various drafts cannot be more than two or three years at the most.

A simple example comes from the very first sentence of the book '. . . the clocks were striking thirteen'. The first draft has instead '. . . a million radios were striking thirteen'. In fact nowhere in the book are radios mentioned, only the telescreen, and we can see here that the invention of the telescreen, one of the most enduring and threatening ideas he created came to him after he first started writing the book. Its origins are not hard to find on the surface—the television system had started up again shortly after the war ended and anyone who was anyone, the inner party, had a set. The idea of having it transmit as well as receive seems to be a genuine invention of Orwell's, one of the few really original science fiction inventions in the book. It is more than likely, though, that his intention here was to satirise the activities of the Thought Police—MI5—and their use of the telephone for monitoring people's activities, which Orwell clearly knew about. In simple terms 'bugging' was almost impossible in the early days of surveillance because the microphones were all bulky and could not be readily hidden. When Julia takes Winston out into the country she takes him somewhere where there were only small ashes around them, explaining 'There's nothing big enough to hide a mike in', and that they were not being bugged. Instead the security services used the ordinary telephone whose handset was rewired so that it became a microphone. It functioned normally when picked up but otherwise acted as a microphone. This method was used extensively during the war years and became widely known, accounting for many people's hatred of the telephone when they realised what had been happening. The danger of a telephone being 'bugged' in the conventional sense, that is, that the calls were being listened to, was irrelevant in comparison to one that had really been bugged.

Orwell's invention of the telescreen simply carried the idea one stage further. It was indeed a brilliant invention which has fathered a generation of surveillance systems, culminating in the present day when most stores and streets, even in a West Country provincial town, are covered by cameras continuously recording everything happening. At the time there must have been a select few who knew very well what Orwell was getting at. The surveillance went a stage further than looking at people's letters which, as we have seen, Orwell had actually been involved in. This kind of activity is perhaps the final degradation of the moral standards of the Victorian age, built up over the centuries which Sir Wilfrid Lawson had warned of.

An example of a theme suppressed was that of anti-Semitism and the problems of the Jewish refugees from Europe who were then trying to get what was to become Israel. At the beginning of *Nineteen Eighty-Four* Winston describes going to a newsreel. The original draft reads:

> Last night to the flicks. All war films. One very good one of a ship full of refugees being bombed somewhere in the Mediterranean. It was full of Jews. The party lowdown was that we gave them a safe conduct and then sent a torpedo plane after it and sank it. Audience much amused by shots of an old fat Jew trying to swim away with a helicopter after him . . .

In the published version all references to Jews are deleted and the text reads:

> Last night to the flicks. All war films. One very good one of a ship full of refugees being bombed somewhere in the

Mediterranean. Audience much amused by shots of a great huge fat man trying to swim away with a helicopter after him . . .

It is obvious that what Orwell originally wrote was a savage satire of things going on in the Mediterranean at the time which clearly did not fit into an account set in 1984. The reference to the party low-down about a safe conduct has echoes of an earlier incident in the war when a ship filled with Jewish refugees going to Canada, the *Arandora Star*, was torpedoed. The boat also had on board a large number of leading fascist detainees, Italians rather than British, and it was widely thought that somehow the Germans had been tipped off about the ship. In fact we now know that Blunt was a Soviet agent and information about the ship could well have been passed to the Germans from Russia, originating from Blunt or one of the other moles. Orwell's suppressed piece of 'low-down' is a relic of this rumour, typical of the time. Orwell had written about anti-Semitism in Britain during the war and his satire may have had a double edge. However, by the time he came to finish the book, knowledge of the concentration camps completely outweighed anger at the activity of Jewish terrorists in Palestine in the public mind, and the text as he originally wrote it, whatever its satirical purpose may have been, was unpublishable.

The diary which Winston Smith began with the account of his visit to the cinema, in the final version of the book, was simply an outpouring of a monologue which he had been carrying in his head for years. In the original draft it was much more than this, a detailed account of all the falsifications that he had carried out in his job at the Ministry of Truth. The original persona he envisaged for Winston clearly had a closer connection to Orwell than that in the final version, for he might well have wanted to keep track of all the material which had been censored in his BBC work, and moved from there to a clerk in the Censorship Department at the MOI who, if he had kept a record, would have been a nightmare to the authorities. Even today they will pursue someone such as Peter Wright who decided to publish what he had been doing. The Victorian principles may have gone by the board but the guilt at what had been swept under the carpet remains. For whatever reason, Orwell changed Winston Smith from a proto-type Peter Wright to someone far more vulnerable, totally dominated by the system he was trying vainly to fight against.

There is a further large group of alterations made to the text in Jura which show how the distancing effect of being there worked positively to enable him to get some way towards the effect he was aiming for. The original draft has many more precise details of locations and people than the final version. A doorman at Victory Mansions, no doubt drawn from life, has gone in the final version. Details of the flat's furnishings, 'a divan bed with a sackcloth cover dyed crimson', a worn green carpet, clearly suggest a real room somewhere and do not appear in the final version. Similarly there is a meeting between Winston and Julia which together with the suggestion that they should have cover names suggests some real incident in Orwell's past. From Jura he was able to loosen the hold past events had on him, and get on with his real purpose which was to satirise the political and social world in which he had been forced to live.

One of the last details decided for the book, its title, is also shown from the drafts to have been more complicated than the usual explanation that he simply reversed the last two digits of the year in which he wrote the book, 1948. The original draft set the book in 1980; this was changed to 1982 and then 1984. The date was 1982, for Julia and Winston first go to the country on a Sunday, the second of May, which was a Sunday in 1982 not 1984. Orwell left a heavily-laboured joke about this in the published version:

To begin with he did not know with any certainty that this

was 1984. It must be around about that date since he was fairly sure that his age was thirty-nine, and he believed he had been born in 1944 or 1945; but it was never possible nowadays to pin down any date within a year or two.

Perhaps the only genuine indication of the reason for Orwell choosing 1984 is to be found here in the reference to the year of Winston's birth. Richard Blair had been born in 1944 and Orwell perhaps intended the warning to be located specifically at a time when his son would be about the age he was when he wrote it. In fact history has moved on to such an extent that the roots of his book have been obscured, as this book shows that they have. His legacy was a practical one in the immense success the book enjoyed, even greater than *Animal Farm*, when he had looked for a sale of only a few thousand copies. And his vision of a golden country and a life far away from the hated London life for his family, where money was of no consequence, was also successful.

CHAPTER SIXTEEN

Nineteen Eighty-Four *in* 1984

The arrival of the year 1984 was greeted by the kind of publicity that the twentieth century has made its own. From editorials in *The Times* to full-scale conferences on Orwell and his masterwork at universities, libraries and arts centres all over the world, the interest was intense. Few commented that if Orwell had decided to call his book *The Last Man* instead of *Nineteen Eighty-Four* the climactic year would have passed without notice and the book itself would never have established the strange relationship that it did with the year whose name it bore—one would say eponymous were it not for Orwell's insistence that the date be spelt out in words, rather than in numerals, in the title. There was an element of chance in Orwell's choice but we can see now that it was not as great as at first appeared. The BBC material and such series as 'A.D. 2000' show the way his mind was moving, following the growing importance of the new scientific inventions from domestic appliances to the atom bomb. Orwell did write to his agent that he would not mind if the book came out in America with its original title; fortunately the response in England swept that idea aside.

The 1984 conferences on Orwell produced a number of books made up of collections of papers and they rivalled other books of essays and comments in the newspapers throughout the year. Most covered the same ground repeatedly, locating Orwell firmly in the contemporary literary and political context. There were few large scale discoveries apart from the BBC material which has led directly to this book. There were, however, numerous insights into particular aspects of Orwell's work. Hsi Huey Liang, for example, in a paper 'The Police State and 1984' printed in *Beyond 1984—The Vassar Symposium*, elucidated one of Orwell's more mysterious biographical references, his statement that Somerset Maugham had been a writer whom he admired immensely, for his ability to tell a story 'straightforwardly and without frills'. Orwell's biographers have passed this statement by, particularly since he said also that Maugham had been the modern writer who had influenced him the most—not a verdict that would sit comfortably with the literary canon of those concerned! Liang drew attention to Maugham's 'Christmas Holiday':

> In this story one of the figures is an idealistic young Cambridge undergraduate living in self-imposed exile in Paris, teaching himself self-abnegation and devotion to a cause so that he might one day command the police of revolutionary England.

Liang points out that the hero catches the spirit of Felix Dzerzhinsky, the Polish nobleman who established the dreaded *cheka*, precursor of the KGB, and whose statues were always the first to be torn down in the revolutions in the Eastern bloc. The suggestion that Orwell's days as a *plongeur* were spent in conscious imitation of Maugham's hero is perhaps far-fetched, of a piece with the idea that he might have been working for MI5 himself. But at least it establishes some link for what may have been intended as a typically Orwellian reference.

At the other political extreme is an example of a collection of essays *Inside the Myth—Orwell: Views from the Left* which epitomises the intellectual bankruptcy of the extreme left and their violent prejudice against Orwell that survived intact from the days of the People's Convention up to the collapse of the Soviet regime. Orwell would have recognised them in a moment. The essays vary in quality. One, by

Antony Easthope, provides genuinely funny relief from the general gloom of studies of Orwell in this genre. There is Freudian interpretation in abundance which culminates in the identification of the crystal paperweight which Winston finds in a junk shop and puts in the room he and Julia share in their few brief days together, as a phallic symbol. The sense of the essay is epitomised in an extract concerning O'Brien:

> In *Nineteen Eighty-Four* O'Brien is the focus for Smith's paranoic sense that everyone is watching him and threatening him. At points in the text Smith's homosexual love for O'Brien [sic!] and his heterosexual love for Julia coalesce in a compromise formation for example when he fantasises that he might use the paperweight [previously identified as a phallic symbol] to smash her skull in or again when he tells her: 'the more men you have had the more I love you'. But for Smith the negative Oedipal trajectory wins out in the end.

Smith's sense of being watched is not paranoia, it is the normal state of things in *Nineteen Eighty-Four*. That is what Orwell was warning against, a warning based on his own knowledge of exactly how much surveillance of this kind went on. No doubt the Stasi were willing to commit people who worried about the files they might be keeping on them as paranoid schizophrenics; it certainly happened in the Soviet Union and it is abundantly plain that it could have happened here. There is always the natural tendency of people who are actually being persecuted to respond with readily identifiable behaviour patterns which point to their believing they are being persecuted! In the old saying in Buffon: 'This animal is dangerous. When attacked it defends itself.'

Perhaps the most interesting paper in this collection is that devoted to literary precedents for Orwell's book, some of which we have already mentioned in passing. Titled 'World Without End Foisted Upon the Future—Some Antecedents of *Nineteen Eighty-Four*', by Andy Croft, it reviews possible sources for the

183

book from the acceptable literary canon whilst paradoxically neglecting to make any serious analysis of Jack London's book, which Orwell specifically referred to, or the extensive literature connected with John Middleton Murry's work or, indeed, the admittedly obscure literature produced by the Brotherhood Movement. Apart from listing a wide range of utopian and dystopian novels from the thirties, none of which have any direct relevance to Orwell's work, the only works referred to which Orwell actually did mention are those already noticed:

> Above all, as he made clear in a comparative discussion about Huxley's *Brave New World* (1932), Orwell's greatest conscious literary debt in *Nineteen Eighty-Four* was to Zamyatin's *We* (1920).

In fact the source cited for this comparative discussion is Orwell's review of *We*, published in *Tribune* in January 1946. The comparison is made between *Brave New World* and *We*. Orwell remarks:

> The first thing anyone would notice about *We* is the fact—never pointed out I believe—that Aldous Huxley's *Brave New World* must be partly derived from it. Both books deal with the rebellion of the primitive spirit against a rationalised mechanised painless world, and both stories are supposed to take place some hundred years hence. The atmosphere of the two books is similar, and it is roughly speaking the same kind of society that is being described, though Huxley's book shows less political awareness and is more influenced by recent biological and psychological theories.

Although Orwell sees Zamyatin's book as being inferior to Huxley's in many respects he does notice political ideas in *We* which are much clearer than anything in Huxley. He refers to Zamyatin's

> intuitive grasp of the irrational side of totalitarianism—

184

human sacrifice, cruelty as an end in itself, the worship of the Leader who is credited with divine attributes.

To move from this to say that Orwell's greatest conscious literary debt is to Zamyatin's book is completely unwarranted. Not only had Orwell already conceived all the essential details of the world of *Nineteen Eighty-Four* before he had even read *We*, but that world is completely different from the hedonistic society that appears in Huxley and Zamyatin. In fact Zamyatin spent much time in England before he wrote *We* and greatly admired H. G. Wells. He hoped to live abroad and become a writer in the mould of Conrad but was not able to do so, although he finally died in exile. His writing owes a great deal to Wells and no doubt Orwell saw this. But he did not derive direct inspiration for his own book from Zamyatin, rather he praises him for the degree to which he has approached what were his own ideas, formed years after Zamyatin's although well before he read his book.

A similar charge, amounting almost to one of plagiarism, is made for Orwell's supposed use of *Swastika Night* (1937) by Katherine Burdekin. There are specific incidents which both books seem to have in common, but they are the kind of incident which also appear in a large number of other books at the time, a photograph which identifies an incident, and so on. Croft candidly admits

> There is no evidence that Orwell ever read *Swastika Night* or indeed that he read any of the anti-fascist novels mentioned above.

In fact the book is of such tangential relevance that it is not possible to tell from the closest reading that there is a connection other than that they can both be described as anti-fascist dystopias. Further, Orwell found it quite impossible to keep silent about books which had interested him or which he had been given to review. There is no trace of any knowledge of Burdekin's book in any of his writings.

A critique of Orwell published in 1984 by Daphne Patai, *The Orwell Mystique: A Study in Male Ideology*, mentions Burdekin's book and that there is no evidence that Orwell had read it, but then goes on to say that he was an inveterate borrower, referring as an example to Jim Phelan's *Jail Journey* as an obvious source. In fact Orwell did review Phelan's book but the idea that he borrowed from him for his account of prison life is absurd. His own experience from both sides of the bars was extensive, and a far more likely source for the cells in the Ministry of Love is the tough interrogation centre we have already described. Indeed all the sources we have located in this book are drawn from the world which Orwell knew and it is quite plain that it was this world and its tendencies that he was attacking with real earnest. He was not engaged in creating some second-hand work of fiction based on tips from others. He admired Zamyatin's book because it struck him as close to the truth as he saw it, and there the matter ended.

As one final example of the kind of 'borrowing' which Orwell has been accused of, but one not noticed by his critics on the left, it is worth reading the very short pamphlet by H.V. Morton *I, James Blunt*. Orwell reviewed the book and referred to it as a thriller written for those who had not realised there was a Nazi danger. James Blunt is living in a Britain that has been conquered by the Nazis and is the victim of oppression. He decides to write a diary as a record of his thought. He describes what life is like with the detail, also found in *Nineteen Eighty-Four*, that large posters of the ruler appear on every hoarding and in every room. The book ends with his inevitable discovery:

> March 13th 1945. I must destroy this diary. It is madness to keep it. No place is safe . . . I can hear someone knocking at the door. I must open the door . . . I . . .
> HERE THE DIARY ENDS.

One is reminded immediately of the incident where Winston Smith no sooner starts his diary than there is a knock on the door and his blood runs cold—he has been discovered already.

In fact it is his next door neighbour asking for his help in unblocking a drain. It is possible to see in James Blunt an early version or inspiration for Winston Smith, but it is also a completely wasted exercise. The actual literary sources are to be found in the writings of John Middleton Murry and others that we have noticed, with the addition of James Burnham, although here again, although Orwell reviewed his books frequently, he does not seem to have either directly borrowed, or to have been engaged in a dialogue with him in the way he did with Murry. It simply is that he noticed him alongside him on the path. As with the other authors who he nodded to, the resemblances between them are bound to be extensive. They were all living in the same brutalised world. Had their vision equalled the strength of his we would know their works now as well as we know Orwell's.

Had the original material in the BBC and the public record office not been discovered Orwell's work would have remained a successful book, with occasional parallels to other situations at the time noticed. The biographies all take this line in one form or another without any detailed knowledge of the world of the BBC and Miniform, the Ministry of Information. They also failed to notice or discover the other key source—Orwell's wife Eileen and the work that she did. Between them Orwell and his wife must have come to a very clear understanding of the quasi-totalitarian systems in operation in wartime Britain. What they knew provides the basic world in which Winston Smith, an employee of the Ministry of Truth engaged in censoring the past as well as the present, had his being. Orwell made his hero one of the faceless censors in the inner recesses of the MOI, on the receiving end of all the pneumatic tubes carrying messages from the front desks, because he epitomised the kind of person who would have to revolt if there was to be any revolt. People from his own world such as Burgess or Empson with their enthusiasms for Basic English or their secret political loyalties would be the betrayers; perhaps Orwell suspected that he too might be on the wrong side. He remarked that Jack London saw the dangers of fascism correctly because there was a streak of fascism in him and perhaps, knowing his own background, he had those fears of himself. It was people such as Winston Smith who might seem to be the hope, and if they failed the only hope left was in the proles.

It is at this basic level that most of the background to *Nineteen Eighty-Four* can be understood, not by reference to other works of literature which Orwell may or may not have seen. The BBC and other ministry canteens are clearly identifiable, and Empson talking on in the basement canteen of the Overseas Broadcasting Department about Basic English or his other linguistic theories can be seen as an exact model of Syme in *Nineteen Eighty-Four*. There may be other private references which are now impossible to capture. The woman at the Ministry of Truth who worships B.B. as her saviour might bear a resemblance to some real person who trembled whenever Brendan Bracken was mentioned, and thanked God he was there to protect his staff when Churchill's wrath descended upon them, but she is more effective as a satirical figure of a kind of bureaucrat that is essential to the working of the system. Parsons closely resembles an old Orwell stock figure whom he had described in his articles, the community hikers who wore shorts whenever they could and spent all their spare time at the community centre. The detail of the dampness of the table-tennis racket handle after Parsons had been playing with it tells us that Orwell knew that world well.

At the other end of the social scale the Chestnut Tree Cafe, with its young hopefuls such as Winston himself alongside the old political heavy-weights, long discredited, stands as a lasting satire of the kind of ambience found at the Cafe Royal, with Kingsley Martin no doubt intended as the epitome of the political has-been. The difference between the canteen and the Chestnut Tree Cafe is, in social terms, exactly that between Winston's worn out mansion block with its view of the Ministry of Truth, and the luxury blocks that looked out on to the park where O'Brien and the other inner party members lived. And in reality Orwell's flat was exactly that degree away socially from those blocks more recently built that looked out on Regent's Park in St John's Wood. The proles lived in slums everywhere. Winston explores those near King's Cross in the original manuscript, although they are less precisely defined in the final version. They remained untouched, with the bombed sites and shored up buildings, for decades afterwards. In some streets, mercifully, the ambience survives up to the present day as anyone walking around the backstreets as both Winston and Orwell used to do will soon discover.

There is a further difficulty in attempting to identify figures in *Nineteen Eighty-Four* as if it were almost a *roman-à-clef*. That one of the female characters in Inez Holden's *Night Shift* wears overalls and has a sash around her waist is suggestive, and that she herself may have worn overalls like that points to her being in some sense a model for Julia. But this only emphasises the limited knowledge we have of Orwell's circle during the vital wartime days. His working colleagues at the BBC and on the magazines have all publicised their memories of him, but others have fallen out of sight. When the author spoke to Mulk Raj Anand in Bombay it was clear that no Orwell scholar had realised that he was part of the close circle of friends around George and Eileen. The discovery of the BBC letters had made this known, and also added another dimension to our understanding of Inez Holden, their mutual friend. But here again the passage of time soon obscured memory; Inez Holden sent Anand copies of her later books as they appeared but with her death the literary world that remembered him and the others grew smaller in real terms, since Eileen and George Orwell died very young; H.G. Wells, an occasional host to them, although Orwell and he quarreled fiercely, also died at the end of the war; and others such as Reg Reynolds, Ethel Mannin, Murry himself, who knew them, often felt that Orwell had deserted what they believed in—pacifism, or the ILP. There were few left alive from his own circle. The result has been a peculiarly one-sided view of Orwell which some of the material here, with that in the BBC archive, will perhaps correct.

It is a paradox of the twentieth century that knowledge does not become greater or more complete than it did in previous centuries just because advances in technology suggest that it should. Some, such as the telephone, militate against the writing of letters: the BBC files now will tell future historians even less than those of Orwell's day.

The most frightening thing in Orwell's predicted totalitarian world is the constant spying, the telescreen that listens to every word, even when you are asleep and watches every movement, or might be watching, all the time. Since the publication of Peter Wright's memoirs we now know that it was not only the Stasi that spied on their fellow citizens. There were always people who knew what was going on and that MI5 used surveillance methods of this kind, but there were not many of them. Orwell's parody would have seemed, indeed, a nightmare of a future world to ordinary citizens. Only the few would know what he was driving at and feel the full force of his satire. By the fifties it was widely known that the Russians would take photographs of people in compromising circumstances in order to blackmail them or publicly humiliate them. Again few would have thought the British would stoop to such levels—it was precisely the sort of thing that generations of Englishmen had been taught was not done, although it was an American who, when he learnt that letters were being opened during the First World War, reacted in horror saying 'Gentlemen do not read each other's mail'. In fact Orwell knew that all these things were being done in Britain during the war and continued after it had ended.

The forty years and more that have passed since Orwell wrote his warning have seen a great levelling in the standards of living in Britain, at least as far as one-time luxuries such as cars, televisions and other consumer durables go, and it is difficult to recall the world Orwell knew. Winston Smith is a member of the party, an elite of a few hundred thousand at most. The inner party would consist of a few tens of thousands. The surveillance and terror that operates in *Nineteen Eighty-Four* was meant for that small number only. The bulk of the population are ignored. The situation in East Germany and Russia was far worse. There it was not just the party members who were spied upon but everyman, unlike *Nineteen Eighty-Four* when being in the party even offered some protection. Mass surveillance in Britain is now possible almost at this level, without any great improvement in technology. Electronic telephone exchanges mean that any phone can be tapped at will without the need for elaborate mechanical operations to fit the taps. The advent of the 'smart card' could soon lead to the 'smart' identity card which would have on it all that the authorities need to know about a person. Medical practices in the south west of England have used such cards for some years and a patient produces a card which is wiped through a viewer to produce, on screen, their case history. If smart identity cards became compulsory, as some government officials have urgently suggested, then anyone stopped would immediately have to produce a card which could be wiped by an officer in his car to reveal all he wanted to know. The stage beyond that, already in use for dogs, is to inject a chip beneath the skin. At the moment the authorities in Britain are only considering this for prisoners and other offenders. This is an Orwellian world that Orwell indeed foresaw but applying to the entire population, not just an elite.

The key phrase always used to justify such ideas is 'The innocent need have nothing to fear'. Whenever that phrase is used in final justification, as it was used in Nazi Germany, communist Russia and no doubt every other totalitarian state since the dawn of history, then infringement of civil liberties is certain and freedom, as it is understood in America, and as it was understood in Britain in the nineteenth century, right through to the days of Sir Wilfrid Lawson, will have passed. The gloss of the consumerist society will not be able to hide what has happened. And the word used to describe this tendency is still 'Orwellian' or, more simply, 'Big Brother'. The justification of the need for such a regime was always, in the past, the fear of communism or invasion, or revolution. With the ending of the cold war and the collapse of the Soviet regime these reasons fall away. What is left is the most human motive of all, the motive of the righteous who have persecuted through the ages: power. As Orwell has O'Brien say when forcing Winston to admit that most absurd untruth, that two and two make five, 'We are the priests of Power'.

Beyond the daily world of wartime London in the BBC and MOI, and beyond the surveillance of the Thought Police (MI5 or their like) Orwell talked about the evolution of the superpowers who would survive in a nuclear stand-off perhaps for a millennia. Ironically it was in 1984 itself that the first tentative moves which presaged the collapse of this arrangement between the powers appeared. They occurred in Germany, both East and West, where people began talking about *Deutschlandpolitik* and the possibility of the reunification of the two halves of Germany. They occurred in America where people began to wonder how much longer the division of the world along the lines sanctioned at the Tehran and Yalta Conferences forty years before could carry on. And they occurred in Britain where the decision to join Europe seemed more and more like a transfer of allegiance from Oceania to Eurasia carried on in very slow motion.

Writing in *Foreign Affairs* for winter 1984/85, Geoffrey Howe, the then Foreign Secretary asked:

> Why, 40 years after the last war, are there still 350,000 American troops on the continent of Europe? Why, indeed, are there 66,000 British servicemen still in Germany? In short if the arch [the Atlantic Alliance] was not there, would we need and want to invent it?

The reason of course was the existence of the superpowers armed with nuclear weapons and a cold war situation which Orwell so brilliantly described in his novel. In the same issue

192

of the magazine Zbigniew Brzezinski wrote an article on 'The Future of Yalta'. He pointed out that Yalta was 'unfinished business' and that the myth of Yalta had directed attention away from its historical significance:

> The myth is that at Yalta the West accepted the division of Europe. The fact is that Eastern Europe had been conceded *de facto* to Joseph Stalin by Franklin D. Roosevelt and Winston Churchill as early as the Tehran Conference (in November–December 1943), and that at Yalta the British and American leaders had some half-hearted second thoughts about that concession . . . The Western statesmen failed, however, to face up to the ruthlessness of the emerging postwar Soviet might, and in the ensuing clash between Stalinist power and Western naivité, power prevailed.

This is *precisely* George Orwell's analysis made at the time. Those who criticise *Nineteen Eighty-Four* because the totalitarian world he prophesied did not arrive in the West, in all its exact detail, overlook both the full arrival of what he feared in the East and the remarkably accurate prediction he made of the overall global situation, and even more that in Europe. For Brzezinski to write an analysis in 1984 which exactly corresponds to Orwell's analysis made nearly forty years before is tribute indeed. There was no satirical intent in what Orwell wrote at this level. This was how he thought the world would develop given the restricted distribution of nuclear weapons. Geoffrey Howe's article was no more than a continuing of that system but, as was said before, in very slow motion. Europe was not united—with Britain detached from Oceania, no longer airstrip one, and now there is a possibility that she might look towards the East, or that the East might look towards her and declare friendship. In the end it was Russia who played the German card by permitting the tearing down of the Berlin Wall and making possible the subsequent reunification of Germany. For the first time since Orwell wrote, the analysis underlying *Nineteen Eighty-Four* no longer holds. His first fears about the atom bomb being widely available have re-emerged with a Saddam Hussein, looking on posters all over his fiefdom like nothing so much as Big Brother himself, possessing the bomb. Brzezinski referred to the myth of Yalta. Satire strips away the myths and delusions that people invent for themselves to make life more comfortable. Swift's *Gulliver's Travels* and his other books did this for his generation. There can be no doubt that Orwell's book performed the same task for our age, even if it has taken forty years for the truth behind the satire to be revealed even partially. No doubt future disclosures will show us more of the world Orwell was warning against. We can hope that the archives of 'the Thought Police', when they are finally opened, will not be on the same scale as those of the Stasi in East Germany. That they must be opened is clear, even if only to prove this hope is not in vain, and that there really was some basis to the claims of truth and freedom for which millions were fighting in the last world war and for which hundreds of thousands of free-born British men and women died.

Orwell's party dictum: 'He who controls the present controls the past' has been the watchword of far too many in Britain and elsewhere, most obviously behind the iron curtain where it existed in all its original vigour. It is a testimony to the strength of the bureaucratic process in Britain that the roots of *Nineteen Eighty-Four* itself still needed to be established half a century after it was written. We can only hope, again, that the process will not need to be repeated a further half-century on, in the year 2020.

Notes

p.3   In an essay in *Tribune* in November 1946 Orwell bore out Potts' view directly: 'Nineteenth-century America was a rich empty country which lay outside the main stream of world events and in which the twin nightmares that beset nearly every modern man, the nightmare of unemployment and the nightmare of State interference, had hardly come into being.'

p.6   Gow referred to two of his pupils who had written unusual books. The quotation here preserves the literal sense whilst deleting the other author.

p.13 The cover illustrated on the jacket of this book was one sent from Franco's Spain. On its reverse it bears the words CENSURA MILITAR. The British censor's label is not so direct.

p.37 The editing was carried out by the publisher and Tosco Fyvel was involved in it, if he did not edit the entire text. Unfortunately he was unable to identify any of the names which have been excised in the existing version.

p.47 The involvement of MI5 in the legal process has continued to the present day. See, for example, Sean Enright and James Morton: *Taking Liberties: The Criminal Jury in the* 1990s (1990), particularly chapter three on jury-vetting.

p.50 The Security Executive was created by Churchill in May 1940 to get to the bottom of the 'Fifth Column' scare. MI5 had a representative on this committee. It was sometimes called the Swinton Committee after Lord Swinton who chaired it.

p.67 The other contributors to *Story by Five Authors* were Inez Holden, E.M. Forster, L.A.G. Strong and Martin Armstrong. All five episodes were published in *Orwell: The War Commentaries*. How Orwell came to know the last two authors has not yet been established.

p.78 Tambimuttu was a much-loved central figure in the wartime

London literary scene, as anyone reading his Festschrift *Tambimuttu: Bridge Between Two Worlds* (1989), edited by Jane Williams, will soon appreciate. The volume contains much valuable information for an understanding of the period. Orwell contributed to his *Poetry London*, see for example his essay on T.S. Eliot in Volume 2 No 7, for October–November 1942.

p.105   The reference to the 'English Gestapo' was made in a letter by a senior official who was considering resignation. In the event he did not do so. Details may be found in the MOI papers at the Public Record Office at Kew; there also may be found details of the intrusion by a censor into a conversation on the transatlantic telephone link between Churchill and Roosevelt.

p.120   . . . *a barbaric ritual.* Restaurant meals were exempt from rationing coupons, there being only a ceiling on price. The restaurants were used extensively by the wealthy when ordinary people had to subsist on their rations, unless they had a subsidised canteen to go to such as that run by the BBC. Eileen was the kind of person who gave away even her own rations.

p.143   Gathorne-Hardy was at Eton at the same time as Orwell and was part of Cyril Connolly's circle at *Horizon*. If Orwell knew him at the time, or heard about Jura through him, via Connolly for example, no evidence of it has yet come to light. The coincidence of Hardy setting a novel on Jura, hitherto unknown, is in itself remarkable.

p.159   The standard source on Lawson is a edited version of his memoirs edited by G.W.E. Russell and published in 1909. The editor points to the epigraph in the book as representing what he stood for—it would do as well for much of Orwell's thought: 'Laws should be adapted to those who have the heaviest stake in the country; for whom misgovernment means not mortified pride or stinted luxury, but want, pain and degradation, and risk to their own lives and to their children's souls.' (Lord Acton) The callous indifference of today's bureaucratic apparat, and their figureheads, shows the validity of this view today with the reappearance of mass unemployment.

p.171   Murry's book was not published until 1948, however its concepts were much discussed. Professor Crick establishes in the latest edition of his biography that Murry and Orwell actually met for the first time since before the war at a dinner in August 1946. Unfortunately his revised edition went to press before the appearance of new information in the present book, which would have been available to any scholar or bibliophile who wished it.

p.189   To the list of names such as Reg Reynolds should be added that of Bertrand Russell. Orwell met him frequently at this time and the dustjacket of the first edition of *Nineteen Eighty-Four* has a leading recommendation from him. This was removed in the first reprint and has not to date been alluded to or explained. It is most likely that it was an indication of this 'real world' audience that Orwell and his publisher envisaged for the book.

Sources

page

2. *The Lion and the Unicorn* p 120.
3. Paul Potts, *Dante Called You Beatrice* p 84.
5. *The Lion and the Unicorn* p 121.
7. Andrew S.F. Gow, *Letters from Cambridge 1939–44* p 54.
13. *Collected Essays, Journalism and Letters of George Orwell* (vol.1) p 49.
14. *CEL* (2) p 386.
17. *Nineteen Eighty-Four* p 112.
21. *CEL* (4) p 590.
22. *CEL* (2) p 165.
23. John Middleton Murry, *Europe in Travail* p 69.
25. *CEL* (4) p 579.
26. *CEL* (2) p 28.
27. *CEL* (2) p 31.
28. *CEL* (2) p 32.
28. *CEL* (2) p 33.
30. *CEL* (2) p 21.
33. Tosco Fyvel.
35. *CEL* (2) p 48.
35. *The Lion and the Unicorn* p 120.
36. John Middleton Murry, *The Brotherhood of Peace* p 13.
36. *Ibid* p 14.
37. *CEL* (2) p 396.
39. *The Lion and the Unicorn* p 121.
43. *NE-F* p 235.
45. Guy Field, *Pacifism and Conscientious Objectors* p 5.
45. *Ibid* p 12.
46. *Ibid* p 25.
48. *CEL* (3) p 435.
50. *Ibid* (2) p 432.

51.   *Tribune,* 20 December 1940.
51.   *Evening Standard,* 8 January 1941.
54.   *CEL* (2) p 463.
56.   *The Lion and the Unicorn* p 89.
58.   *CEL* (2) p 164.
58.   Ibid 2 p 161.
63.   *Orwell: The War Broadcasts* p 112.
64.   *Ibid* p 223.
64.   *Ibid* p 111.
67.   *Ibid* p 227.
72.   *Ibid* p 283.
74.   *Ibid* p 53.
76.   *Ibid* p 299.
77.   *Ibid* p 57.
79.   *Ibid* p 57.
82.   *NE-F* p 45.
85.   *Ibid* p 45.
85.   *OWB* p 215.
88.   *NE-F* p 42.
88.   *OWB* p 61.
91.   Francis Williams, *Nothing so Strange* p 260.
91.   *Ibid* p 180.
94.   *OWB* p 61.
94.   *CEL* p 29.
95.   Cited in *Orwell: A Life* p 491.
95.   Dustwrapper of first edition of *Animal Farm.*
98.   *CEL* (3) p 459.
98.   *CEL* (4) p 520.
101.   *Ibid* (3) p 209.
101.   *Ibid* (2) p 172.
102.   *OWB* p 122.
102.   *CEL* (3) p 118.
106.   Cited in *Orwell: A Life* p 457.
109.   *CEL* (3) p 169.
110.   *Ibid* p 168.
111.   *Ibid* p 189.
112.   A number of letters and memoranda relating to the publication of *Animal Farm* are cited in *Orwell: A Life* p 452f.
113.   *Ibid* p 455.
115.   *CEL* (3) p 207.
119.   *Ibid* p 228.
120.   *CEL* (2) p 400.
123.   *Orwell: The Authorised Biography* p 416.
126.   *CEL* (3) p 454.

129.   *Ibid* p 407.
130.   *Ibid* p 224.
131.   *CEL* (4) p 55.
133.   *CEL* (3) p 420.
133.   *CEL* (4) p 151.
134.   *CEL* (3) p 374.
136.   *Ibid* p 177.
136.   *CEL* (4) p 94.
138.   *Ibid* p 185.
139.   Reuters report, dateline Moscow.
148.   *Dante Called You Beatrice* p 76.
152.   *CEL* (4) p 439.
160.   *Ibid* p. 58.
161.   Interview with Mulk Raj Anand, Bombay 1984.
168.   *CEL* (4) p 25.
169.   *Ibid* p 26.
170.   *Ibid* p 26.
170.   *CEL* (3) p 240.
171.   *CEL* (4) p 36.
173.   John Middleton Murry, *The Free Society* p 44.
173.   John Middleton Murry, *The Brotherhood of Peace*, p 6.
174.   *Nineteen Eighty-Four* (the extant manuscript) p 112.
180.   *Ibid* p 11.
182.   Liang Hsi Huey, 'The Police State and Nineteen Eighty-Four'
       p 109.
183.   Antony Easthope, *Inside the Myth* p 270.
184.   Andy Croft, *Inside the Myth* p 210.
184.   *CEL* (4) p 96.
184.   *Ibid* p 98.
185.   Croft, *Inside the Myth* p 210.
186.   H.V. Morton, *I, James Blunt* p 56.
192.   Geoffrey Howe, *Foreign Affairs* Vol.63, No2, p 330.
193.   Zbigniew Brzezinski, *Foreign Affairs* Vol.63, No2, p 279.

Bibliography

BBC (publishers): *Summary of World Broadcasts* (SWB).

Belloc, Hilaire: *The Servile State* (1912).

Bramah, Ernest: *The Secret of the League* (1907).

Brzezinski, Zbigniew: 'The Future of Yalta': see *Foreign Affairs*.

Burdekin, Katherine: *Swastika Night* (1937).

Calder, Ritchie: *The Lesson of London* (1941).

Craig, Alec: *The Banned Books of England* (1937).

Croft, Andy: 'Worlds Without End Foisted Upon the Future' in C. Norris (ed.): *Inside the Myth* (1984).

Easthope, Antony: 'Fact and Fantasy in *Nineteen Eighty-Four*' in C. Norris (ed.): *Inside the Myth* (1984).

Empson, William: *Seven Types of Ambiguity* (1930).

Field, Guy: *Pacifism and Conscientious Objectors* (1945).

Fletcher, Charles R.L.: *Edmonde Warre* (1922).

Forster, E.M.: *Passage to India* (1924).

Forster, E.M.: Introduction to *The Banned Books of England* by A. Craig

Gathorne-Hardy, Robert: *The Wind and the Waterfall* (1938).

Gow, Andrew S.F.: *Letters from Cambridge 1939–1944* (1945).

Hedley, Peter and Cyril Aynesley: *The D. Notice Affair* (1967).

Hitler, Adolf: *Mein Kampf* (1939).

Howe, Geoffrey: 'The European Pillar', in *Foreign Affairs*.

Holden, Inez: *Night Shift* (1941).

Huxley, Aldous: *Brave New World* (1932).

Kenworthy, John Coleman: *From Bondage to Brotherhood* (1894).

Koestler, Arthur: *The Yogi and the Commisar* (1945).

Lazar, Richard G. and Menahem David Lazar (eds): *Beyond 1984—The Vassar Symposium* (1985).

Laski, Harold: *Faith, Reason and Civilisation* (1944).

Liang, Hsi Huey: 'The Police State and *Nineteen Eighty-Four*' in Lazar, R. G. (ed.) *Beyond 1984* (1985).

London, Jack: *The Iron Heel* (1908).
London, Jack: *The People of the Abyss* (1903).
Morton, H.V.: *I, James Blunt* (1942).
Muggeridge, Malcolm: *The Thirties* (1940).
Murry, John Middleton: *The Brotherhood of Peace* (1940).
Murry, John Middleton: *Europe in Travail* (1940).
Murry, John Middleton: *The Free Society* (1948).
Norris, Christopher (ed.): *Inside the Myth: Orwell, Views from the Left* (1984).
Orwell, George: The most useful biography is Bernard Crick: *George Orwell: A Life* (1992). Unfortunately this most recent edition omits the invaluable first outline of *Nineteen Eighty-Four* which appears in the 1982 edition used here. 1991 saw the publication of Michael Sheldon's *Orwell: The Authorised Biography*. There is a wide variety of editions of the texts mentioned here. The final standard edition will be that edited by Professor Peter Davison.
Orwell, George: 'AD 2000'. A radio series edited by Orwell.
Orwell, Sonia and Ian Angus, (eds): *The Collected Essays, Journalism and Letters of George Orwell* (1970).
Russell, G.W.E.: *Sir Wilfrid Lawson* (1908).
Russell, Leonard (ed.): *The Saturday Book* (1944).
Silone, Ignazio: 'The Fox', a radio adaptation published in W. J. West (ed.): *Orwell: the War Broadcasts* (1985).
Soley, C.: *Radio Warfare: OSS and CIA Subversive Propaganda* (1989).
Struve, Gleb: *25 Years of Soviet Russian Literature* (1944).
Swift, Jonathan: *Gulliver's Travels* (1726).
Wells, H.G.: *The Shape of Things to Come* (1933).
Wells, H.G.: *The Sleeper Wakes*.
Williams, Francis: *Nothing so Strange: An Autobiography* (1970).
Zamyatin, Evgeny: *We* (1920–1). Orwell appears to have read the first French edition.

Newspapers and Periodicals

The Adelphi, ed: John Middleton Murry; *Brotherhood; Daily Herald; Daily Worker; London Evening Standard; Foreign Affairs* Vol 63. No 2.; *Horizon,* ed: Cyril Connoly; *Manchester Guardian; Modern Quarterly; New Statesman,* ed: Kingsley Martin; *Oban Times; Partisan Review; Poetry London,* ed: Tambimuttu; *Polemic,* ed: Hugh Slater; *Politics; Time and Tide; Tribune.*

Index

206